INGE MORATH HOMMAGE

Cover Image:
Inge Morath, Wedding Celebrations,
Magnum Office New York, 1962.
Photo by Wayne Miller

Isabel Siben and Anna-Patricia Kahn

INGE MORATH
HOMMAGE

Schirmer/Mosel

My mother was an elusive and fascinating person to me as a child. She was very private, deeply emotional, modest, elegant, and very giving. She was wounded. She was intrepid. She was a fiercely dedicated mother. She was also a tremendous artist.

As I saw it growing up, Inge hailed from a terrible, mythic past. She had been forged in a cauldron of the deepest evil, had lived in the hottest part of hell—Nazi Germany—and she bore the internal marks of having seen into the Belly of the Beast all her life. Yet one story about that time seems to me to say the most about her character. In 1945, at twenty-two, living alone in Berlin to finish her studies while her parents worked in Salzburg, Inge had splurged on a small bunch of violets, bought from an old woman on the street. Just then, the air raid whistle sounded. Hearing the bombers approach, Inge ran to shelter along with other desperate people. Convinced she would soon be rained on by explosives, she absurdly held the bunch of violets over her head, as protection. Once she made it to safety, she realized how silly that instinct had been. Yet this gesture betrayed her essential self. Inge believed in beauty. It was a kind of religion for her. She often used to murmur, "Beauté, mon beau désir…" Perhaps, having witnessed so much ugliness as a young woman, she turned to beauty, and more specifically to beauty in art, and the power of the artist, as a sign that human beings were still capable of creating something whole, something beautiful, and therefore good. As a photographer, she was fascinated by artists; her seductive and spritely demeanor melted away their defenses. She understood the demands of big, fragile egos. Yet what all her work—from portraits of famous writers and actors, to women in the streets of Iran, or elderly people playing chess in the park—has in common is a deep sense of geometry. The pictures are beautifully composed by an instinct honed through a life-long study of great art.

Having been taken to the Nazi exhibition of "Forbidden Art" by her scientist mother as a child, Inge had long believed that, far from being frivolous or decadent, art is essential, and often contains the last shreds of hope.

I did not realize until I was an adult that Inge was training me to be a visual artist as she raised me. The trips to museums to look at paintings, leafing through photography books, occasionally dissecting her own more successful images—looking for the Golden Mean, making me understand the power of triangles—the nearly mystical geometry that anchors an image, more deeply than sentiment or theme—all of this was being funneled into my little mind without fanfare. As a mother, Inge was not one for rules or punishment; she taught by example. Her self-discipline was legendary. She learned Russian and Chinese well enough to read the poetry and engage in conversation in both languages before attempting to penetrate these cultures as a photographer. When she took a nap, it was on the bare linoleum floor of her studio, surrounded by her beloved German Shepherds, who dozed, guarding her.

No words can unravel Inge Morath's complex, mysterious conundrum of a persona. Yet we have her photographs, which speak of her empathy, her lack of narcissism, her curiosity about other human beings and cultures, and her deep hope that art could be a candle against the darker elements of human nature.

Rebecca Miller

I trust my eyes.

1

Ladies and Gentlemen,

During the Second World War I went to school and later to University in Berlin.It was a difficult time,it was the time of my youth and my memories are topsy turvy,many-layered,in and out of focus. What I will be trying to do here,is to follow the experiences and events which made me into a person who trusts her eyes and, finally became a photographer, a profession of which I not only never dreamt but hardly knew existed.

I am a native of Austria,my parents were scientists who worked in different laboratories and universities, often changing residences from year to year and country to country. My first schoolyear was spent in a french village school run by nuns, and since our parents did not think this at all unusual we children found it quite normal.

My family owned two cameras:one, a Contax, belonged to my mother. It was mounted on top of a microscope in my father's chemical laboratory where she worked as his assistant. She used it to photograph cell-structures, which she tinted with scientific accuracy but with a certain artistic flair. My father used them in his lectures. To me they were abstract pictures which I liked as such, but having no scientific bent, they left me unmoved. The other camera was a large format box and belonged to my grandfather. He had a tripod and a black cloth under which he disappeared for lengthy periods of time while my brother or I

Inge Morath

I TRUST MY EYES

Ladies and Gentlemen,

During the Second World War I went to school and later to University in Berlin. It was a difficult time, it was the time of my youth and my memories are topsy turvy, many-layered, in and out of focus. What I will be trying to do here, is to follow the experiences and events which made me into a person who trusts her eyes and, finally became a photographer, a profession of which I not only never dreamt but hardly knew existed.

I am a native of Austria, my parents were scientists who worked in different laboratories and universities, often changing residences from year to year and country to country. My first schoolyear was spent in a French village school run by nuns, and since our parents did not think this at all unusual we children found it quite normal.

My family owned two cameras: one, a Contax, belonged to my mother. It was mounted on top of a microscope in my father's chemical laboratory where she worked as his assistant. She used it to photograph cell-structures, which she tinted with scientific accuracy but with a certain artistic flair. My father used them in his lectures. To me they were abstract pictures which I liked as such, but having no scientific bent, they left me unmoved. The other camera was a large format box and belonged to my grandfather. He had a tripod and a black cloth under which he disappeared for lengthy periods of time while my brother or I sat for him, decoratively arranged but bursting with impatience on fountain rims and other hard seats until we finally heard the liberating click. If I had been possessed of any objectivity I could have agreed that the treatment of light in these photographs was quite exquisite, but the captured moment seemed to me void of any interest; there I was sitting on a fountain rim that had nothing to do with me. There was nothing surprising or mysterious here, in contrast to the photographs in books borrowed from my parents' library, especially the ones we were only supposed to read when we were older. Paintings exercised a similar attraction, presenting something not quite explained in a conventional form. I never tired of looking at paintings in waiting rooms, living rooms, and my grandparents' and aunts' and uncles' bedrooms where reproductions of Boecklin and Feuerbach played enigmatically on my imagination. My mother loved Duerer and the Barock in general. Naturally we went to museums, but I have no memory of modern, let alone avant-garde works.

But I did have my own encounter with the Modern. Before we moved to Berlin we lived for a few years in Darmstadt in an apartment situated just a few minutes away from a hill called the Mathildenhöhe. On its crest was an artists' colony founded by the Grand Duke of Hesse who had commissioned the architect Joseph Maria Olbrich to execute the buildings. Olbrich created an astonishing ensemble of houses, gardens, studios and a five-fingered tower, built to dominate the land-scape and celebrate an archducal wedding—all in his own Art Nouveau-inspired style. An older Russian chapel commemorating some other archducal event formed a bizarre contrast to the clear lines of the new Art Nouveau buildings. Under the five-fingered wedding tower strange reliefs representing—as far as I remem-ber—naked women playing musical instruments were scattered inside a dense grove of plane trees whose grey and white peeling trunks looked strangely alive. The encounter with the Mathildenhöhe was my first im-portant visual experience, I still recall endless details. Other memories of this time are of visits to the theater, of seeing my first opera, "Mignon," which made me cry a lot, of Indian students of my father's who lived a while with us and cooked their own food, told fantastic stories about their country and considered everybody else rather barbarian. There was also an extravagant dancer friend, who had been performing with Harald Kreuzberg and, more important, left us a collection of jazz records.

Pretty soon, the new order of the now firmly established Nazi regime drew a heavy curtain over this childhood. Naturally I was not quite aware that most things that I had found beautiful soon would not only be taboo but declared to be destructive alien influences on the German mind. Towards the end of the Thirties we moved to Berlin where my father directed a research laboratory specialising in wood chemistry and my mother, as always, worked with him as his assistant. I was registered in the Luisenschule, a red brick building in the Ziegelstrasse near the Bahnhof Friedrichstrasse, commuting almost 2 hours per day first by bike, then by train, as my mother had fallen in love with a house outside the city that stood quite isolated in a big garden. Later we moved to Wilmersdorf, just in time for the bombs. Now the atmosphere was becoming more and more oppressive: books that always had been standing in the front row of the bookcase wandered to the back, and the jazz records disappeared. We were told that denunciation could be dangerous and my impetuous mother, whose reactions were based more on spontaneous feelings than political thought now only mentioned in small circles of friends how simply ghastly she found the brown colour of the SA Uniforms. The word "forbidden" took on serious new dimensions, and then came the word "entartet"—degenerate.

I personally owe my first encounter with the avant-garde to the exhibition of "Degenerate Art" first organized in 1937 by the Nazis to denounce modern art. Circulating all through the country it displayed reproductions of the "infamous" paintings derisively displayed in school corridors to instill in us obligatory feelings of contempt and hatred. I found a number of these paintings exciting and fell in love with Franz Marc's *Blue Horse*. My technique was to stare at the painting long enough to remember it in all its details. Only negative comments were allowed and thus began the long period of keeping silent and concealing thoughts. But out of this suppression a more intense way of visual observation became a habit. Faces were open books, eyes started to communicate what mouths did not dare to say anymore. I cannot remember much about the illustrated papers of this time as the fateful year of 1939 approached. Photographs were almost exclusively used for propaganda and I had no interest in looking at them. The Third Reich had almost completed the occupation of its own country, and the regime's demand for blind obedience—when they could not get adulation, became crushing.

World War II began. Life became more and more joyless. There still were some excellent theater productions and concerts, but at home one was not allowed anymore to listen to foreign radio transmissions, and if one dared to do so it was under a blanket, for hostile ears were everywhere. I passed the Abitur (final school examination before university), then did service in a daycare center for workers' children. If one of them complained his or her father would threaten us "intellectuals," sometimes with blows. Then came 6 months of *arbeitsdienst*—labor in the countryside. I was sent to Grossborken, a thoroughly miserable place in Eastern Prussia. Luckier classmates landed nearer Berlin, but it was impossible to determine where and why the die that determined the next months of your life was cast. The "successful completion" of this grueling work meant a certificate of good conduct which was a pre-requisite for admission to the University. Among the roughly 50 girls in the camp, only two of us wanted to continue our studies. The leveling of the spirit and the formation of a national socialist type were the aims of our leaders. The boss was a woman named Clemens who had a sharp nose for non-enthusiasts. She would check out our underwear, and finding that I was wearing underwear that I had brought from home instead of the scratchy handouts gave her reason for riding herd on me every day. She measured the length of the skirts of our ungainly uniforms from the ground up and weighed us once a week—we were not supposed to lose weight despite the food. Reading of books was considered an unworthy activity but as I did it anyway I had to regularly clean the latrines. I did not mind, at least they left me alone there. We had to sing lustily when we marched out at dawn to go to the different farmers we were assigned to but they were as unenthusiastic about our presence as we were about working for them. I sat many hours in a dark cellar, the trap door in the kitchen floor above me firmly closed, cutting the eyes off old potatoes. The farmers loved to push my arm deep into a bucket filled with dung meant for the roots of turnips we were planting. Their favourite sport was to watch a city girl cleaning out the pigsty and being chased by an irate sow. "We'll show them" they said. The other girls came from the surrounding countryside so that we two seemed alien to them, which put us under suspicion. What saved us was that they were quite illiterate and needed our services to write their letters. Which did not, however, stop them from listening for any suspicious remark which they could report to Ms. Clemens, thereby putting themselves in a favourite light as she was eager to gather incriminating material which would make our acceptance at the university difficult. Our mail was censored, and it became impossible to write a true word home. I just hoped that my mother would read between the lines. The technique of concealing one's thoughts grew more refined, as did, by necessity, the power of observation. One of the minor "leaders" who had sympathized a bit with us, was dismissed. In protest a couple of us accompanied her to the station. Punishment ensued at once, there was no room for the slightest expression of non-conformism. But all this can only suggest the almost unbelievable atmosphere of this time, the time of adolescence, my formative years.

Returned to Berlin, I managed to get matriculated at the University in spite of my not exactly flattering *arbeitsdienst* certificate. The Berliners, thank God, often had a mind of their own. At the same time the bombs started falling. The war claimed its first victims from my family: my three cousins were killed, each on a different front, within a relatively short period of time. They had been the dear playmates of my youth, and during our vacations in Austria, I fell in love, alternately, with two of them.

They were hardly twenty years old and I remember a long late night talk with one of them, the most handsome one; he was wearing the amethyst ring of his new fiancée, and said that some of his comrades felt that they no longer knew what they were fighting for, but that they were carrying on even if the battle seemed lost. I never saw him again, and his brother had been killed shortly before on the Western Front.

I studied where I could find a quiet space, in the University and the Underground stations that served as air raid shelters. I did not join the studentenschaft (student's organisation) and one day, in the subway, one of the professors, his name was Pfeffer, bent down and whispered into my ear "We'll get you yet." (A few years after the war, on a visit to Germany with my American husband, this man approached me on a ferry and asked me to help him get a new book of his published. Of course, there was no mention of his wartime threat.)

My father, a fighter pilot in World War I, was drafted into the reserve of the Air Force. My brother was shot down during one of his first flights in his fighter-bomber by the English over the Mediterranean and remained on the "Missing" list until news came that he was in a prisoner of war camp in Egypt.

My mother still worked in the laboratory. We made occasional trips to the countryside to buy potatoes and anything else we could get. Once someone denounced us, I don't know why, and we were left without rationing coupons for a couple of weeks. Three different images from this time remain especially vivid in my memory.

After a bomb attack, which we had waited out in a neighbouring Underground station, my mother and I walked home and arriving at our house found that the front wall had collapsed and was hanging in raglike shreds with the rooms now open to the street. On the ground floor, in the smashed rubble covering my father's desk, stood our most fragile possession: a vase made of ruby glass in the shape of an urn that my parents had brought back from Venice and that we children were not allowed to touch for fear it would break. Amid all that destruction it stood undamaged. It was like a ray of hope. Now we shook the dust and rubbish off our beds and slept. The night was pleasantly warm.

The second image is of a performance of the Second Part of Goethe's *Faust*. Gustav Gründgens played Mephistopheles. He wore a tight leather cap like a second skin over his bald head and he spoke one of the long monologues hanging backwards over a rock, his lips painted dark red.

The third image is of a leaflet—it was towards the end of the war and the British had dropped it during the night. It showed a photograph of mountains of shoes, shoes of men, women and children, and the description under it said that all the owners of these shoes had been killed in the concentration camp of Maidanek.

It was this photograph that obliterated any doubts that all the whispered rumours about the unspeakable atrocities of the concentration camps were true.

Shortly after that I was drafted for factory service in Tempelhof. I received a grey identity card on which was marked "Until the victorious end of the war." I worked on an assembly line and turned screws. The Berlin women who were regular workers were helpful and sometimes let me have a piece of their sandwiches. Most nights were spent in air raid shelters. One night after the all-clear had sounded a time bomb exploded, a horse bolted and the cart it drew ran me over. My left leg was lacerated. Miraculously, a car stopped, behind the wheel a doctor on his way home. He picked me up and drove me to my shelter and he said "just put some coaldust in the wound. It will heal, we have no more medicaments." It did heal and a slightly black scar remains on my shinbone.

The Russians were practically outside Berlin. One night, after a heavy bombardment, convinced they would soon be marching in and that chaos would reign, I started to walk in the direction of Austria. Who could still track me down in all that tumult? My parents had gone to Salzburg months ago. Some soldiers were about to blow up a bridge outside Berlin but they still paused to let me pass. There seemed to be no control over people leaving the city. One soldier gave me a piece of sausage and soon I was not walking alone anymore. Everybody seemed to be in flight. Some trains still ran so one was still looking for railway stations. All platforms were densely crowded, but occasionally I managed to hang onto a train, gaining a few kilometers, until some low-flying spitfires hit the train and the passengers ran out, throwing themselves flat onto the ground until the attack was over. Many people were coming in from the East, but not many words were exchanged as even now, in the death throes of the Third Reich, silence was considered prudent. There was no water to drink, no water to wash with, no place to relieve oneself. I decided to drown myself in a river but a passing soldier pulled me off the railing and yelled at me that I had no right to do that, that he had come from Russia where he lost a leg and that the whole thing was going to be over soon. He accompanied me into Salzburg but I could no longer recall where our house was, and he walked me up and down street after street until I saw a familiar doorknocker and ran to it and when the door opened there was my mother. I turned to invite the soldier in but he had simply vanished. I was amazed; he had gone like an angel.

Later I did not photograph wars, I could not. But I did several works about and with refugees, symbolizing the consequences of all wars just as the photograph of the shoes of Maidanek symbolized the brutality of all concentration camps. I had made it to Salzburg and found my parents but I was sick from exhaustion and hardly noticed the arrival of the American Third Division and the announcement of the end of the war. We ate out of soup kitchens and made the welcome acquaintance of peanut butter, given to us by the American soldiers who had quarters in the same house.

My father came on an ad in the local paper that had again started to be published under American auspices: the Information Services Branch was looking for interpreters. We all needed to earn money, so I went and landed my first job in the ISB feature section in the Berggasse in Salzburg. I learned not only to translate information that arrived from the States but also to use it as material for small articles to be written for distribution to the press.

Roughly a year later, in 1946, the feature section moved to Vienna where we worked in big offices in the same building where the *Wiener Kurier* was being published. My work grew more independent, and I became familiar with the ground rules of journalism. At the demarcation line between the American and Russian zones which we had to cross when we went from Vienna to Salzburg, the Americans used a large syringe to shoot DDT down our necks and the Russians endlessly scrutinized our identity papers, a frightening procedure when stories were circulating of people who had been taken off the train and were never seen again.

In Vienna, along with a colleague of mine, I was assigned a room in the flat of the widow of a Nazi official. We had to share the bathroom with her and there was no love lost between us. The Americans provided our lunches, a lot of spam and dried peas. But life had begun again and everything seemed possible once more. We could read the formerly forbidden books, see the new French, English and American plays, paint fingernails red and above all to say what one thought, loud and everywhere. I started to write some little radio plays for the Red White Red network, worked as an editor for a literary magazine called *The Optimist* and promptly folded, but helped me meet writers and artists. Hans Weigel, Ingeborg Bachmann, Ilse Aichinger became friends. Arnold Keyserling lectured about all kinds of wisdom, especially oriental, in his studio. The first meetings of European Intellectuals took place in Alpbach, organised by Otto Molden. Viktor Frankl, a founder of Existentialism, let me sit in on lectures in which he analysed people who could not re-enter a normal life after the experience of the war. He himself had survived Auschwitz, where his wife and other family members were killed, and he saw it as his task to teach the survivors in his words "to say YES again to life."

I found a new job as Austrian Editor of *Heute* magazine, published by the Americans in Munich. One of my tasks was to find photographers to take pictures for the stories I was to propose. For the first time I started to study photographs and picture stories, especially in the now available *Life* magazine, which was in its heyday and published great picture essays. My problem was that the photographs I came across in my searches simply did not inspire me. Then came the day I was introduced to Ernst Haas, saw his photographs and was delighted. We started to work together, did some stories about fashion and other subjects that did not really interest us, under the mistaken assumption editors would like them. Finally we threw ourselves into a story which we thought nobody in all probability would like as it was

downbeat, spending days and nights at the railway station where the transports of Austrian prisoners of war were arriving from Russia. Each transport was greeted by a crowd of anxious people holding up photographs of missing family members, hoping to get some information. The tragedy of war was written all over the faces.

We took the story to Warren Trabant, our editor in chief, who, after seeing our earlier efforts, had only told us: "This is dreadful. But I think you are talented, keep going." But this time he was enthusiastic, published Haas's photos and my text and sent copies to Robert Capa who, in 1947, had founded Magnum Photos. Capa cabled "Come to Paris." It was July, 1949.

We packed a suitcase each and departed, never suspecting that we would never again return to Vienna for any length of time. Inside my suitcase was the old Contax my mother had taken off her microscope and given to me. This camera accompanied me for nearly three years more without ever being used. I still only wrote about my observations, in my own diaries as well as magazine stories and now worked also on captions and short texts for the stories sent back from various parts of the world by Magnum photographers.

As a writer I was frequently accompanying Ernst Haas and others on story trips but in the office I embarked on a new and thrilling activity: the editing of contact sheets which the absent photographers could not tend to themselves. Contact sheets are the diary pages of photographers, the editor following each pressing of the button trying to do justice to the decisions taken through the viewfinder, carefully weeding out weaker pictures. Henri Cartier-Bresson was still travelling in the Far East and his contacts fascinated me with their sequence of pictures showing the rigorous pursuit of an event in clear geometric compositions. I think that in studying his way of photographing I learned how to photograph myself before I ever took a camera into my hand.

In 1951 I married an English journalist and moved to London. I felt quite at sea. England is very different from the Continent. Subtle, incomprehensible codes of behaviour constantly assaulted me for I moved in Shrewsbury, Eton, Oxford circles. It was easy for a foreigner to fall on his face and I often found myself silently observing rather than talking. I suddenly had time on my hands and walked for hours alone through London. To my surprise I began to see more and more things that I felt should be photographed. I called photographers I had met, but they were rarely interested as I only offered ideas but no real assignments. One day we went to Venice on a short vacation. It rained when we arrived and I found the light astonishing, the dark silhouettes of the wet passers-by seeming choreographed against the marble walls. Finally, I couldn't stand the frustration anymore and called Capa in Paris and asked him to send a photographer as I was certain that in this weather one could make a great picture essay about this city born out of the water. Capa simply said: "You are an idiot, my dear. Who is going to pay for this? Besides, it will stop raining before anybody gets there. Why don't you finally take a picture yourself?"

What exactly made me do it, I don't know, but I went back to the hotel room, got the old Contax, had a film put in in a camera shop (I didn't yet know how to do that), declined the advice of the shopkeeper that the signorina should wait, tomorrow there surely would be sunshine. That was precisely what I did not want; for one thing I had worked with photographers shooting in the rain. Studying the directions packed with the film, which said "Cloudy: 50ᵗʰ of a second at 4," I quickly repaired to the spot I had selected as a lookout and set myself in the place of the not materialising photographer. I stood there, looked through my viewfinder and when people, columns, pigeons, presented themselves in a rhythm I would have liked to see on a photograph, I pressed the shutter. It was instantly clear to me that from now on I would be a photographer, I finally had found my language. As I continued to photograph, I became quite joyous, I knew that I could express the things I wanted to say by giving them form through my eyes. I remembered what Henri Cartier-Bresson had written somewhere: "A good photograph is made when the inner vision behind the closed eye corresponds with the vision of the open one behind the viewfinder in the moment of pressing the button." Returning to the hotel I practiced without a camera, with one eye closed and one open watching the street, trying to figure at what moment I would take a picture.

It turned out that changing professions took some doing. Who would have bought one of my photographs—I who was known for never taking one? So for the time being I kept my plans secret. I placed an article here and there, went a lot to the theater and the superb London museums. Naturally I was on the lookout for someone who could teach me more about photography. I had heard of Simon Guttmann, once the director of the famous German photoagency Dephot, the first to practise the idea of the photo essay. Under the photographers who had worked for Guttmann at the time, was Robert Capa—but I did not know that yet. In 1942 or 43 Simon Guttmann arrived in England via Switzerland and France, and became adviser to the best English illustrated magazine of the time, *Picture Post*. He also founded his own agency, Report, and had several photographers working for him, one of whom advised me to try and see if he would take me as an apprentice. Warned that he was highly critical and difficult, I was terrified as I went to my first meeting with him in his tiny, unimaginably crowded office in Oxford Street. All I had to show were the three contact sheets of my first films taken in Venice. He looked at them, not making the slightest commentary. Then he asked: "What do you want to photograph and why?" I mumbled something to the effect that I was mostly interested in people, in the variety of their lives, and I added that I was certain that after the life in the isolation of Nazism and war I felt I had found my language in photography, or at least the best way to express what I felt I had to say. He told me I could start to work with him.

I spent several weeks typing his letters, on Saturdays I answered his phone and dropped coins in his gas heater to heat his shaving water, things his strict Judaism forbade him to do on the Sabbath and occasionally I swept the rooms, careful not to topple over any of the piles of newspapers on the floor. "When are you going to teach me how to photograph?" I finally ventured to ask. "That's exactly what I am doing," he answered impatiently. "Why don't you really pay attention to what I say in my letters? I only gave you the ones addressed to editors or photographers to type. Everything you can learn about photography and how to make a picture story is in them." And he was right. From then on in the evenings he would send me out into the streets to use my Contax and make stories about opening nights, exhibitions, inaugurations, a fire in Smithfield market and other events. Another photographer who already had worked with Simon Guttmann for a while had a small darkroom in which I learned—from handbooks he recommended—how to develop films and make enlargements. Everything one produced there one had to show, and fear of Guttmann's sharp criticism inspired effort. Later I spent many nights in the darkrooms of master technicians and observed how they produced the kind of enlargement that are ideal for the photographer: they manage to reproduce the photographers' intention in the moment of shooting, recreating the eye's balancing act between light and shade.

After a few months Simon Guttmann declared that I now could go and work on my own. He had been pleased by a story he had sent me to do in Paris about the inspection of the Horse Guards by a melancholy Prince of Wales. My new passion helped me to leave a marriage that had been kind of a mistake from the beginning. To take pictures had become a necessity and I did not want to forego it for anything. For a while I stayed with two girlfriends in London, bought a second hand Leica, sold some photos under the unintentionally Swedish-sounding name Egni Tharom—my name turned backwards. I began sending pictures to editors with my texts under that name. Finally I got enough money together to return to Paris, where I knew cheap hotels, had old friends and where the Magnum office was. I had decided to make a picture essay that was good enough to show to Robert Capa and put my cards on the table.

My subject would be the workmen priests—*prêtres-ouvriers*—who worked mostly in factories in Paris and other French cities, with the aim of being missionaries in their own country, spreading their faith and helping the poor. I managed to get an assignment and a small advance from the editor of a Catholic weekly. It turned out a difficult undertaking for I had to get permissions from father superiors and the priests themselves were at first reluctant due to the delicacy of their work. More, while the Cardinal of Paris approved their mission the Vatican emphatically did not. We discussed how best to show the importance of their work and the contribution of a dedicated group of helpers who had founded small centers in poor neighbourhoods, distributed food, cared for the old, helped unwed mothers. The technical conditions were lousy, it was dark everywhere in the factories, the rooms, on the way to and from work. I learned then how to make use of small amounts of light for it would have been far too disturbing to bring lamps. But it's always best if after a while people forget about your presence.

After one rather hungry month of work I was ready. The editor of the Catholic magazine was pleased and I went, carrying copies of pictures and text, to Magnum where I had made a date with Robert Capa. He looked at everything, liked the text and finally said: "Who took the pictures, I like them." "I did." "You?" "Yes, I want to be a photographer." Capa was the most generous of all photographers. He now let me photograph the small assignments that came in that did not interest the big boys. The first one was a "Concours des Roses" in the Parc des Bagatelles. Fee $100. Older gentlemen in dark suits judged roses, smelling them, scrutinizing shapes and sizes. First I stood there and did not know how to go about getting exciting stuff out of such an unheroic theme. But when you really start to look all of life is interesting. It was roughly at this time that Henri Cartier-Bresson's book *Images à la Sauvette*—in English *The Decisive Moment*—appeared. *Images à la Sauvette* is derived from "se sauver," to rather hastily depart rather like a street vendor at the approach of the eye of the law. It was not unlike a photographer who, head in the air and pretending other preoccupations, sidles away leaving the passers-by puzzling "Did he take a picture or not?" Henri gave a great imitation of this procedure. Among the photographs in this book was above all one that taught me how to photograph life and forget about aesthetic prejudice. It is a picture of people having a picnic at the bank of the Marne River. All are quite corpulent, the women in petticoats most emphatically so. But it doesn't make sense to describe photographs; I was just deeply impressed by Henri's simplicity of approach and the refinement of his vision in capturing the simple pleasure of working people enjoying a day off and a meal outdoors.

The other photographers got used to the fact that I had joined their ranks. Robert Capa sent me to London to do a story on the set of *Moulin Rouge*, a film John Huston was directing in Shepherds Bush Studios. Originally he meant to do this story himself, so when he passed it on to me he warned, "You'd better be good." I had never been in a film studio before. The only other photographer present was Eliot Elisofon who was advising on certain colour effects and was famous. I tried to watch him but the first day he mostly sat in his chair. An assistant gave me some advice: not to cast a shadow, not to stand on cables or get in the eyeline of the actors. Not to press the shutter when the sound is running. John Huston, who noticed my bewilderment, decided to be of help, especially after I had confessed to his vast amusement that I absolutely had to bring back some good stuff but only had one roll of film—(film was hard to get then and Capa said I should borrow some from Elisofon, but he was not forthcoming.) Huston promptly got me three more rolls, and occasionally waved to me when he thought I should get in there and take pictures.

It worked out fine, I got nice layouts and even a couple of double pages in several European magazines.

I had been very lucky to become part of this group of photographers, distinguished not only by the excellence of their work but by their spirit. After so much suffering they were determined to work at the shaping of a better postwar world. Robert Capa who had become famous for his photographs of the Spanish Civil War and the Allied landing in Normandy for *Life* magazine, founded this photographers' co-operative in 1947 together with Henri Cartier-Bresson, David Seymour, George Rodger, Bill and Rita Vandivert. They called the new agency "Magnum"—a Latin name announcing the ambitions of this group that consisted of one Hungarian, one Pole, one Frenchman, one Englishman, and two Americans—but that also, especially for Capa, symbolised that big bottle of champagne that would be used to celebrate future success. Not being in the pay of magazines, with a minimal office structure, each photographer in the group was free to choose his own stories. Liberated from the domination of the big magazines and commercial agencies, Magnum set about on its new way of creating photojournalism. One of Capa's most important decisions had been to insist that the negatives remained the property of the photographers. However, this harmony of intentions did not mean stylistic unity, quite on the contrary; everybody took the pictures he wanted to take in his own style.

But Capa made the big decisions. He loved a rather extravagant life style and facing the photographers he would often sigh, "If I were rich I would keep racehorses—as I am not, I have you instead." He found work for us all by playing Gin Rummy with movie makers and editors in Zürs, Kitzbühel or Deauville. He was extraordinarily quick to discover the potential in people and knew how to challenge them to do their best work. An anecdote illustrates the atmosphere of these years. Cartier-Bresson wrote—"In 1951, when I returned from a three-year trip to the Far East, I expected to find a nice sum of money in my account. My pictures of China and India had been published all over the world. But Capa said: 'We are nearly bankrupt. So I had to use your money in the meantime, but we'll get it back.' When I showed my surprise he said, as always: 'Just cool it.' And then he reeled off about ten different ideas for stories I should do. Eight of them were no good, number nine was interesting and number ten excellent. So I just picked up my camera again and went to work."

Robert Capa decided that before he sent me off on big photo essays on my own I should work for a while with Henri Cartier-Bresson as researcher, translator, apprentice. Henri and I travelled mostly in Europe, talking little about photography and much more about the paintings we looked at everywhere, about books and the surrealists whose way of thinking had influenced him very much. He also had a keen interest in politics and the French paper *Le Monde* was required reading.

When I did not have to work for him, I photographed what I came across. At that time one had to stick a viewfinder on top of the camera to decide what lens to use. Henri gave me one produced by Leitz called Vidom which he himself often used. It went from 35 to 135 mm, and according to the distance of subject from camera, one could adjust the parallax. What delighted Henri about this viewfinder was that looking through it you saw things on the opposite side of where they really were, and better yet with a turn you could see everything upside down. After some trial and error, the eye got used to judging a whole scene in this rather abstract way. Thus, it taught one to watch a continuous movement inscribing itself on the existing geometrical pattern so that one might press the shutter at exactly the right moment, or at least what one judged to be just that. Naturally, this can in the end only be intuitive. "Your compass must be in your eye", said Henri.

I also learned a lot from watching. It was always the photographer who had to move, a slight bend of the knees or a turn of the head changed the perspective, the meeting points of lines. Slowly all this becomes second nature and one focuses on the events.

In the Magnum office we all looked at our work quite critically, brutally so sometimes. There was no tolerance for explanations about the difficulty of getting a certain shot in order to excuse shortcomings.

My first big assignment came from *Holiday* magazine: a photo essay about Soho and Mayfair. I returned for a while to London and found it exciting to now transform into pictures the impressions and experiences of a life I had lived there without a camera.

Then Capa sent me to Spain, he had invented a new series called "Generation Women" on which most Magnum photographers worked in different countries. "It's a good story" he said. "Your Spanish lady is a lawyer, defending poor women in divorce cases—quite a feat in Franco Spain. Besides, Spain is the right country for you."

He was right. Spain became one of the places to which I returned many times. I quickly learned the language and felt in my element, it was almost like entering a dream one had had many times. I loved the people, they let me photograph them, but they also wanted me to listen to them, to tell me what they knew, so that they and I told their story together. Without knowing the language I would have missed much and since then I have tried to learn the languages of the countries in which I planned to spend much time working, including Russian and Mandarin Chinese.

On May 25th, 1954, Robert Capa was killed by a landmine in Vietnam where he was photographing the French Indochinese war for *Life* magazine. It seemed unthinkable. Then, two days later came the news that Werner Bischoff had died in a car accident in the Peruvian Andes. Robert Capa's brother Cornell left *Life* magazine and joined Magnum, and David Seymour took over as

bureau chief. Two years later he was shot photographing the Suez crisis.

We went on working, determined to keep going in their spirit: do good, responsible work, be tolerant of different ways of seeing, cherish friendship and love life. Since then many new photographers have joined Magnum. Talented men and women working each in his own way, they go on creating photographic essays that stand on their own next to written reportage and television in a world in continuous flux with an omnipresent thirst for information.

For me, the time of the big stories and far-flung trips had begun. For a while I worked in the Middle East, especially in Iran, where in 1956 some contemporary ideas started to make an inroad, at least in Teheran. In the countryside, the mullahs reigned. It was difficult to photograph there as a woman. I had been lucky to find an Armenian driver who knew the country, warned of possible gaffes and pitfalls, and showed me how to properly wear a chador to hide my cameras. I dreamed of following the silk route to China from Iran but that did not work out. I still had to wait many years to photograph in China.

Work never stopped, it was wonderful: I followed the Spanish trail to Mexico and South America, did a story on gold and diamond mines in South Africa, to name a few. In between we all worked on stories about big motion pictures on locations from the Andes in Argentina to Hollywood. Some of the essays became books, one of mine was about refugees from the last of the Russian ones in Germany to the Palestinians in Gaza. This work I did together with Yul Brynner for the United Nations.

At the end of the Fifties I got it into my head to follow the Danube from the source to the Delta to find out more about this big river of my homeland, a river of frontiers, linking so many civilisations and countries. I am repeating this trip now, and again there will be refugees cruelly forced to leave their homes on account of war.

In Paris, a new art magazine, *l'Œil*, was founded by Rosamond and George Bernier. One of the editors was Robert Delpire, with whom I had already made a book about the bullfights in Pamplona. Leafing through my contact sheets he had noticed the number of portraits I took whenever I found a chance. He liked them and I started to do a series of portraits of artists for the magazine, as well as a book on Venice with Mary McCarthy.

I had added a big format Linhoff to my equipment which I used for the reproduction of paintings. I prepare myself for a portrait with the same care as I prepare myself for a trip to a new country: I look at the paintings or sculptures, read the books or plays, see the films of the artists I am to meet. It is good to be prepared as the encounter itself is short and spontaneous and a facial expression is as fleeting as a shadow. I need to photograph people in their places of work or where they live, in the surrounding they created for themselves, in the old quest of capturing something of their essence by inviting them to be themselves. It took me a while to be able to find the harmony in faces that at first seemed difficult and to do it justice. One of the great regrets of my early working time is that I never took a picture of my admired friend Ingeborg Bachmann. I was afraid that in a photograph I would not be able to render the somewhat hazy expression that made her face beautiful. I think that now I could do it. One dreams of the pictures one missed.

Since the end of the Fifties I worked more and more frequently in the United States. I had long wanted to meet the caricaturist Saul Steinberg whose drawings in the *New Yorker* had, already in my Vienna time, sharpened my eye for America. I made a date to meet for a portrait and he received me in his house in Manhattan with a brown paper bag over his head, on which he had drawn a caricature of himself. In the kitchen, he had hung a whole wall full of more brown bags, all of them with self-portraits in a number of different moods. We started a great game: he drew more pictures of all kinds of Steinbergian characters on paper bags and I found people to pose wearing them. It was interesting to observe how quickly the sitters' bodies assumed positions that corresponded to the expression of the mask. A study in impersonation—how am I presenting myself to the world today?

In 1962 I married the American playwright Arthur Miller. My travelling slowed down, but I soon found that photographic discoveries can be made in one's own backyard. A writer's rhythm is different, he takes his time to think and choose his words. For us, a missed moment is lost forever. But over the years his way of thinking about an event has helped me to find other ways of seeing. The stories he told about the old timers amongst whom he lived in his first years in Connecticut were a splendid incentive to take a close look at my immediate surroundings. Our first book was called *In the Country* and combined our ways of discovering.

In the following thirty years I travelled, sometimes with Arthur or alone, to many more countries which I longed to see, especially Russia and China. On account of his efforts to help writers in political difficulties—for years he was the International President of PEN—we met with many artists whose dangerous situation could often be alleviated by focusing international attention on their plight. Needless to say, I also got a chance to take many portraits. Walking with him in unfamiliar streets it was often the writer's curiosity that led to photographic opportunities in events that at first looked barren of such interest.

Sometimes I travel alone, and the discomfort which so often accompanies taking pictures is even more unmitigated: rising at dawn or earlier, with miserable means of transport and long hours of waiting for this or that reason, the work can be hard. But I have learned how to combine my life with my work which is as it should be. Meanwhile our daughter writes and directs movies, belonging to the generation which seems to be

tied by an umbilical cord to the moving picture. But even she, I am happy to say, needs stills.

Photography itself is changing. New techniques make the stamp we applied to the backs of our pictures in the old days—("No cropping, no airbrushing") look rather touching. Digital techniques can change photographs without leaving a trace of the manipulation, people who have never seen each other can stand together. Finished is the time, for example, when you knew exactly where in an official group picture a disgraced official had been retouched out of existence, leaving a hole, in one case a hat suspended in air which the censor had forgotten to eliminate. I am having fun learning some of these new techniques, but for me they remain rather cold techniques and don't become a passion. But I am still curious, I still trust my eyes to look at life and help celebrate it.

And now, I will just show a few photographs as this is my work, which you, the spectator have to complete by looking at it.

INGE. PORTRAITS AND SELF-PORTRAITS

1   ISRAEL. Jerusalem.
Inge Morath. Self-portrait. 1960.

2   Danube River. Inge Morath.
Photographer unknown. 1959.

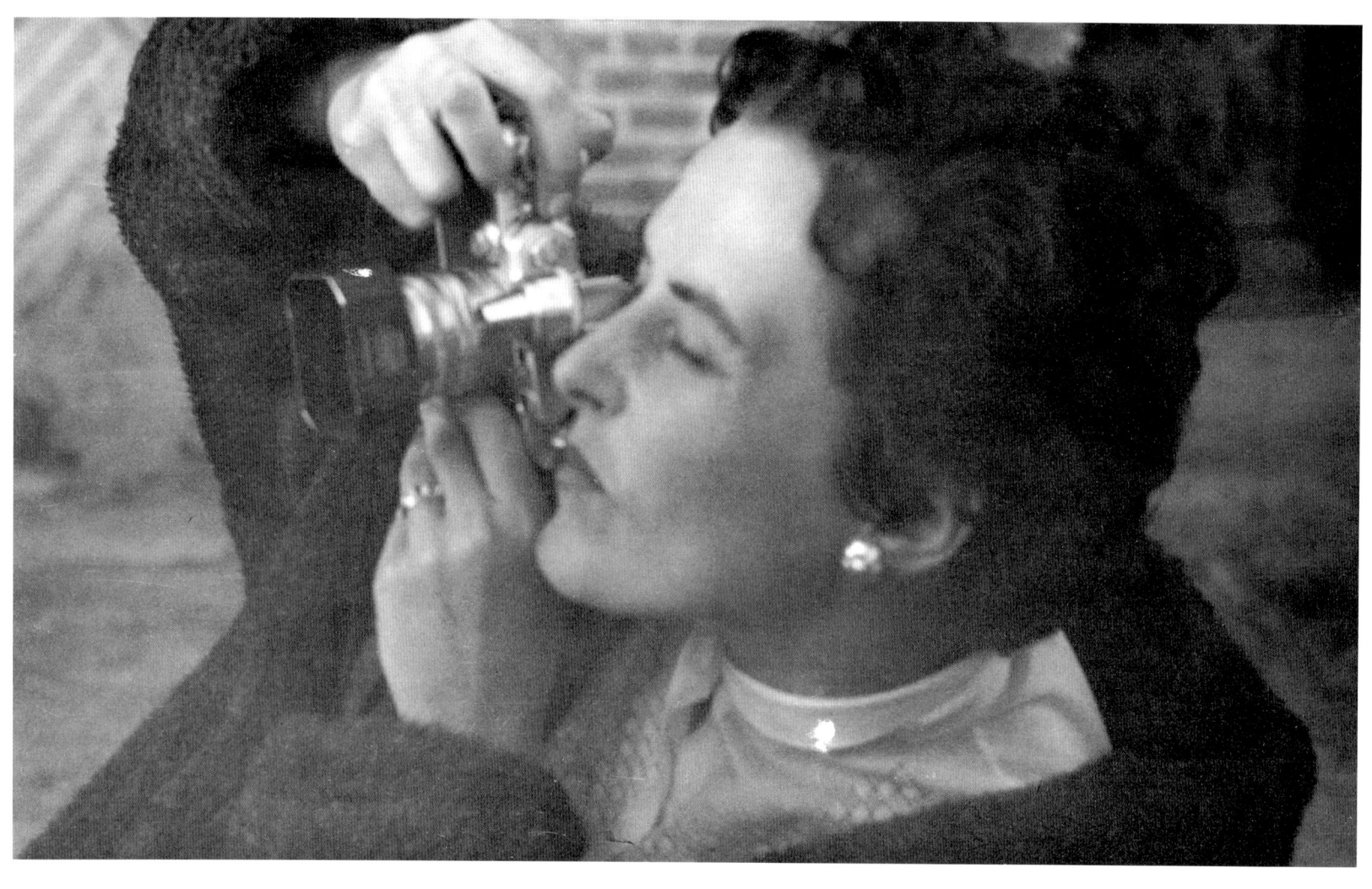

3–7   ENGLAND. London.
Inge Morath adjusts her Leica camera.
Photographer unknown. 1954.

8 FRANCE. Paris. Inge Morath.
Photographer unknown. 1955.

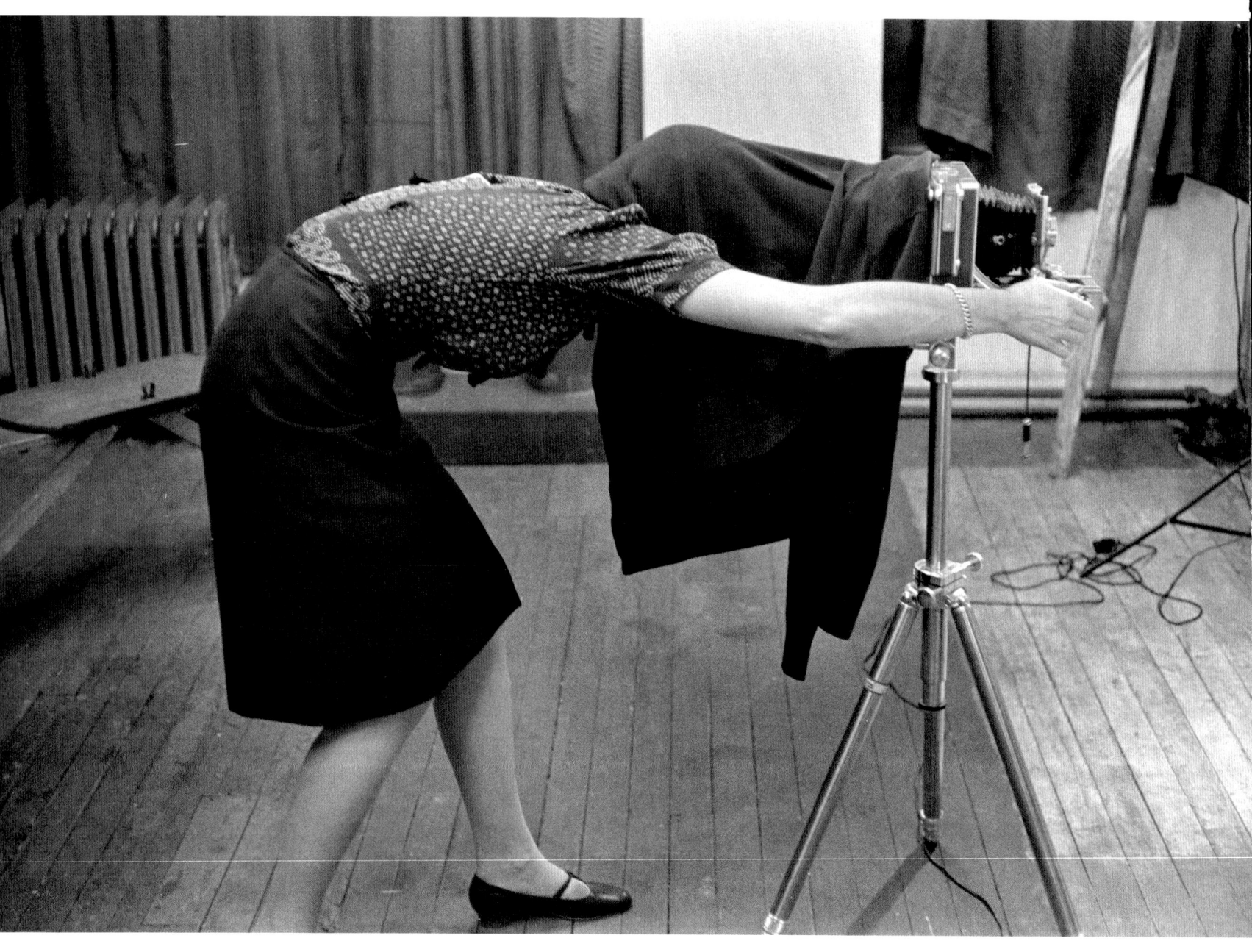

9 USA.
Inge Morath. Photograph by
Henri Cartier-Bresson. 1960.

10 USA. Arsdale. Inge Morath during
a visit with writer Mary McCarthy.
Photographer unknown. 1956.

11   FRANCE. Paris.
Inge Morath. Photograph by
Henri Cartier-Bresson. 1959.

12   AUSTRIA. Vienna.
Inge Morath. Photograph by
Yul Brynner. 1958.

13   IRELAND. Inge Morath dancing
with director John Huston in his home.
Photographer unknown. 1954.

14–18   IRELAND.
Director John Huston performing a
Charlie Chaplin dance in his home. 1954.

19   USA. Cherokee, NC. Inge Morath.
Photographer unknown. 1960.

20   USA. New York, NY.
Inge with Linda the Llama.
Photographer unknown. 1957.

21   USA. New York, NY.
A Llama in Times Square. 1957.

22   USA. New York, NY.
A Llama in Times Square. 1957. (Detail)

23   USA. New York, NY.
A Llama in Times Square. 1957.

24   USA. New York, NY.
Linda the Llama with her owner. 1957.

European Distribution

Photographed by Inge MORATH, MAGNUM PHOTOS.

CAPTIONS

1. Linda, the Lama, rides home via Broadway. She is just coming home from a television show in New York's A.B.C. studios and now takes a relaxed and long-necked look at the lights of one of the world's most famous streets.

2. Linda lives in Manhattan like a real New Yorker and when she comes home they neighbourhood kids say hello before she walks into the front door of her foster parents: Lorraine and Bernhard d'Essen.

3. If one walks behind Linda through the front door, one soon finds out that she is by no means the only extraordinary foster child of the d'Essen's. There are, just to greet their master at the breakfast table: Jester, the Persian cat, Lulubell who is a mixture and always try to sit on Linda's back, Linda herself, Deborrah, the great Dane and Lady, a ~~wolfhmxxx~~ Russian Wolfhound.

4. Linda, the lama, has a sip of coffee. She first tried to get at Bernard D'Essen's cup, eventually settled for whatever drops she could lick from the saucer. Linda loves coffee.

5. Lorraine and Bernard D'Essen pose for a family portrait. Some of their animals are missing, but a good deal of them after some persuasion decided to pose. From left to right: Jester, a Persian cat; Linda, a Lama; Deborah, a Great Dane. Mrs. Lorraine D'Essen; Lola, a basset hound; Bethseba, a pig; Tilana , a tiny Yorkshire Terrier. Bernhard D'Essen; Abner , another basset hound, father of Lola's puppies and partly invisible; Victoria, a very nice cangaroo and Lady, a Russian Wolfhound.
   All these animals are not only wonderful pets, they also are, thanks to the training and understanding guidance of their owners, top models and stage and television performers.

6. One morning a miniature bull arrived as a new inmate at the D'Essen's house. Victoria, the cangaroo, daringly took up first contact with this strange looking animal.

7. Mortimer, the new miniature bull is introduced by Lorraine D'Essen to some members of the family, the two basset hounds Lola and   and Deborrah, the great Dane.

25   Captions sheet:
USA. New York, NY.
"A Llama in Times Square". 1957.

AT HOME with Mrs. D'Essen, llama lies in the living room amid dogs and Victoria the kangaroo.

High-paid llama in big city

The urbane llama taxiing through New York's theater district at right is Linda, a popular model for photographers who pay her $100 a sitting to lend distinction to their pictures of high fashion. She owes her success to Mr. and Mrs. Bernard D'Essen, whose Animal Talent Scouts provides well-bred actors for TV, advertising and Broadway. To teach manners to dogs, kangaroos and wombats they raise them like children in their home, (*above*). One of their most difficult jobs: teaching Linda not to spit in the eye of demanding photographers.

FEATURED PIG who plays Salome in Broadway musical *Li'l Abner* sniffs police horse on sidewalk.

LONG-NECKED LINDA ogles from taxi window on way to make appearance on a TV show. She likes riding in cars and after a brief look around usually settles down on the floor of taxi and takes a nap.

27   Contact sheet:
USA. New York, NY.
A Llama in Times Square. 1957.

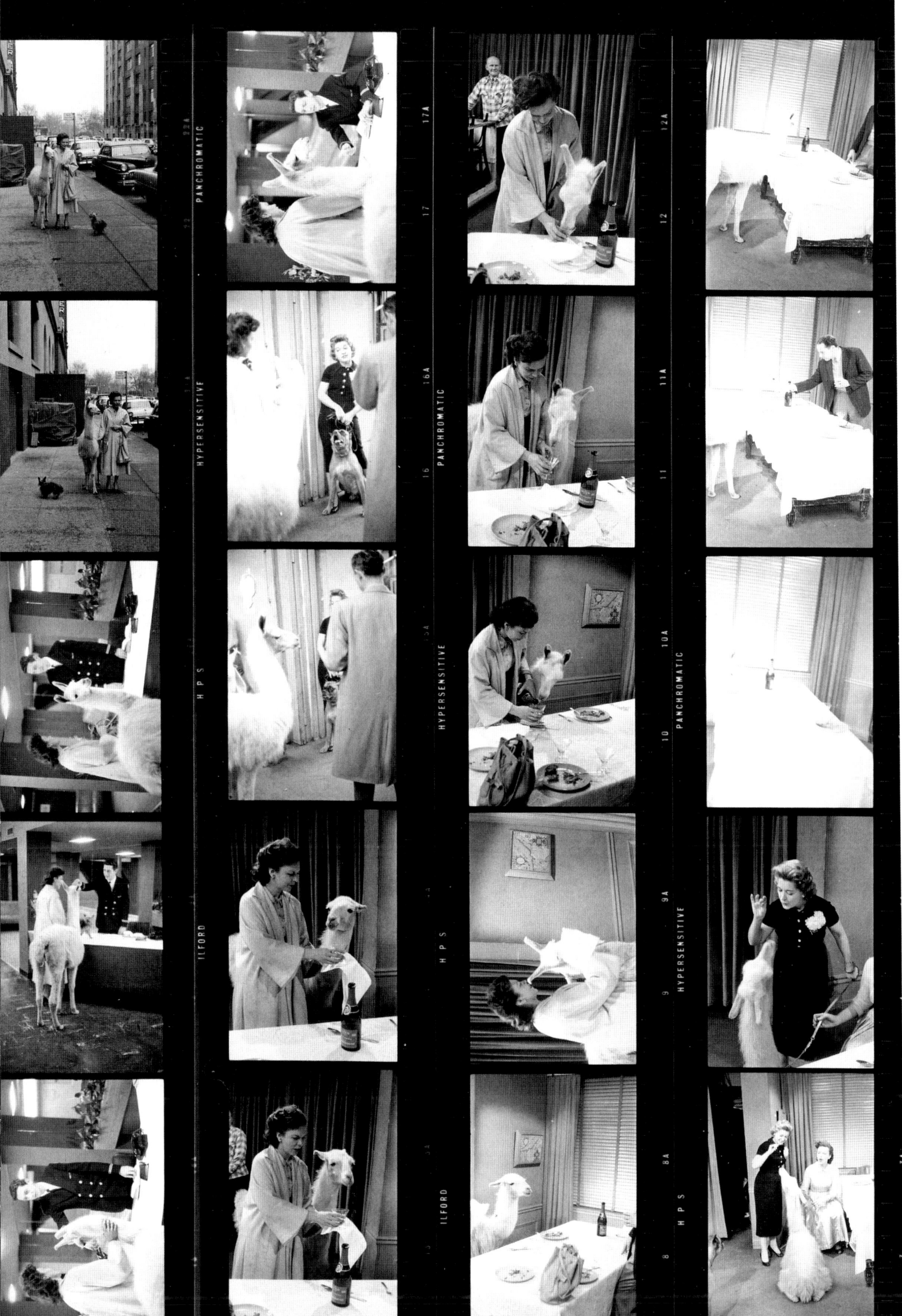

Pages 48–49:
28   ENGLAND. London.
Mrs Eveleigh Nash at Buckingham
Palace Mall. 1953.

29–30   ENGLAND. London.
Mrs Eveleigh Nash. 1953.

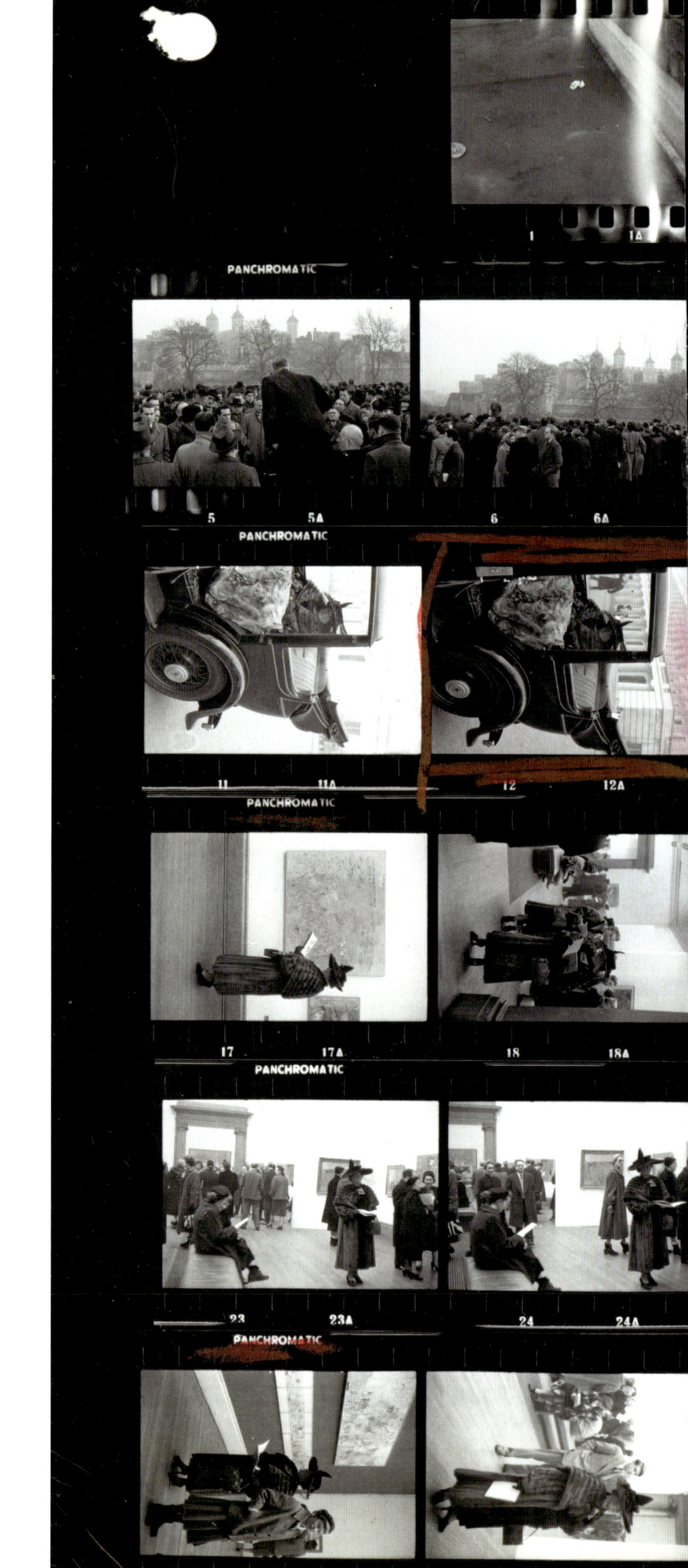

31 Contact sheet:
ENGLAND. London.
Mrs Eveleigh Nash. 1953.

2   2A   3   3A   4   4A

ILFORD   HP 3   HYPERSENSITIVE

7   7A   8   8A   9   9A   10   10A

ILFORD   HP 3   HYPERSENSITIVE

13   13A   14   14A   15   15A   16   16A

ILFORD   HP 3   HYPERSENSITIVE

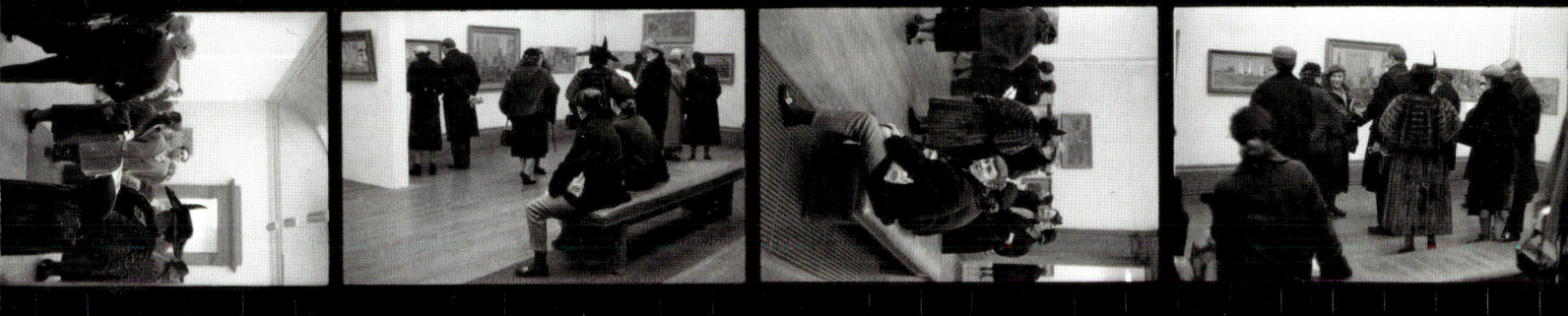

19   19A   20   20A   21   21A   22   22A

ILFORD   HP 3   HYPERSENSITIVE

25   25A   26   26A   27   27A   28   28A

ILFORD   HP 3   HYPERSENSITIVE

32–37   USA. New York, NY.
Untitled (from *The Mask Series*
with Saul Steinberg). 1961.

38   USA. Long Island, NY.
Arthur Miller peeks out from
behind a Saul Steinberg mask, 1962.

NEW YORK CITY, LONDON

39   USA. New York, NY.
Window washers at Rockefeller
Center. 1958.

Pages 60–61:
40   USA. New York, NY.
Visitors on top of Rockefeller
Center. 1958.

41   USA. New York, NY.
Merry-go-round in Central Park. 1960.

42   USA. New York, NY.
Chess players in Washington
Square Park. 1958.

43   USA. New York, NY.
Ice skaters at Christmas Show
on Madison Avenue. 1958.

44 USA. New York, NY.
New Year's Eve in Time Square. 1958.

Pages 66–67:
45   USA. Brooklyn, NY.
View of the Brooklyn Bridge. 1961.

46   USA. New York, NY. Actress Nancy
Berg hurries along 5th Avenue. 1956.

47 USA. New York, NY.
Lady and her dog at 5th Avenue
and 87th Street. 1958.

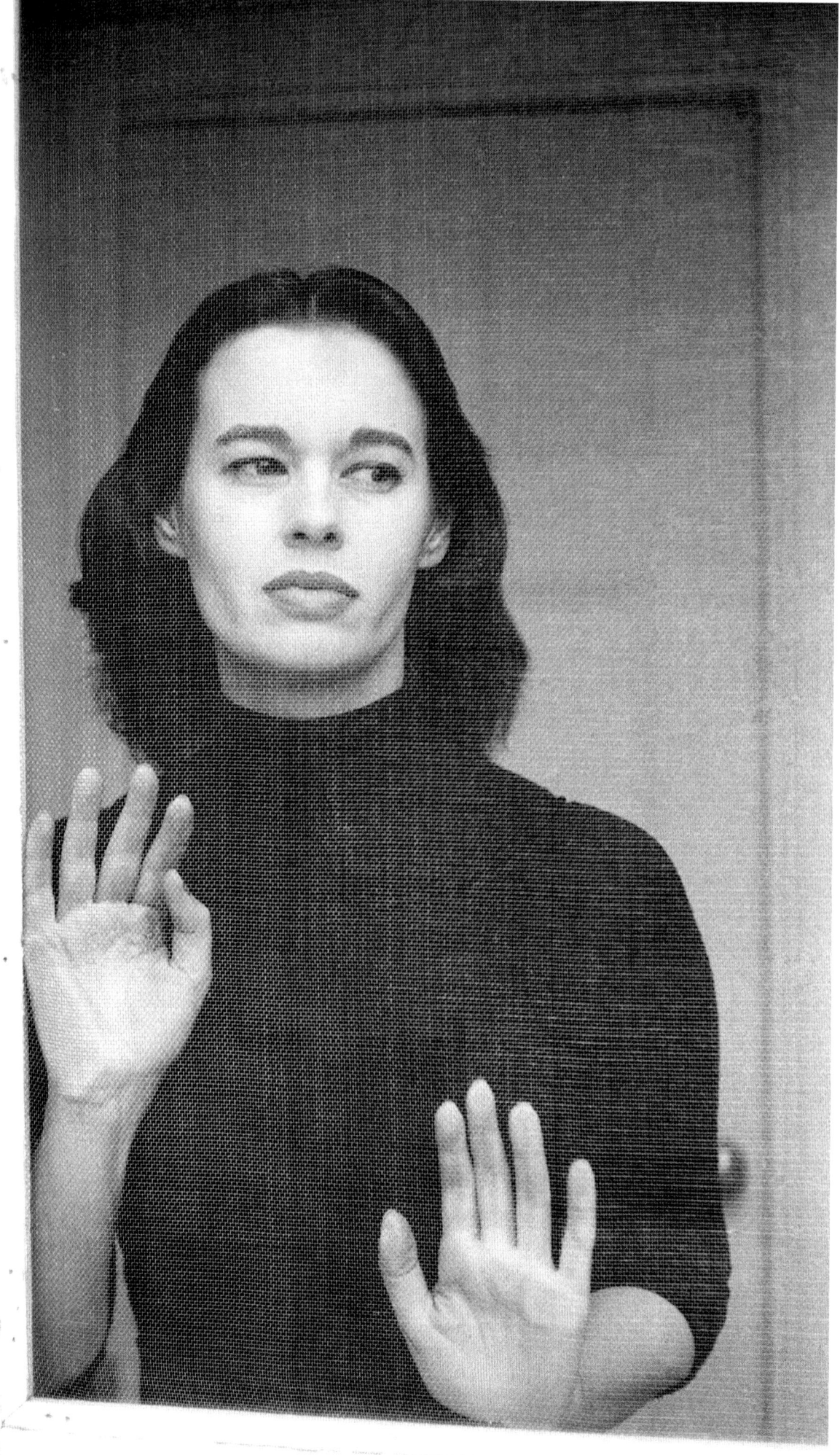

48–50 USA. New York, NY.
Gloria Vanderbilt. 1956.

51 USA. New York, NY.
Beauty class at the Helena
Rubinstein Salon. 1958.

52   USA. New York, NY.
Helena Rubinstein Salon. 1958.

53   ENGLAND. London.
Fog on the River Thames. 1954.

54–55 ENGLAND. London. 1953.

56–57 ENGLAND. London. 1953

58   ENGLAND. London.
Street corner. 1954.

59–60   ENGLAND. London. 1953.

61 ENGLAND. London. 1953.

62 GERMANY. Munich.
Maximilianstraße, photographer
Henri Cartier-Bresson. 1953.

63 USA. New York, NY. Magnum Photos
meeting in Cornell Capa's house.
Bruce Davidson, Henri Cartier-Bresson,
and Dennis Stock. 1962.

64   FRANCE. Paris. Ernst Haas and
Henri Cartier-Bresson at a Magnum
meeting. 1958.

65 ENGLAND. London. Novelist
Salman Rushdie with playwright
Arthur Miller in a restaurant. 1993.

66   FRANCE. Paris.
Poet Jacques Prevert, 1958.

67   FRANCE. Paris.
Writer André Malraux, 1956.

68 USA. Boston, MA.
Novelist John Updike. 1996.

69   USSR. Moscow. Playwright
Friedrich Duerrenmatt and actor and
director Maximilian Schell. 1987.

70 CUBA. Havana.
Writer Gabriel García Márquez. 2000.

71   USA. New York, NY.
Writer Philip Roth. 1965.

72 USA. New York, NY.
Poet Pablo Neruda. 1966.

73 USA. New York, NY. Arthur Miller,
Saul Bellow, and John Steinbeck
at the PEN club meeting. 1966.

74 USA. New York, NY.
Composer Igor Stravinsky on his way
to Columbia Recording Studios. 1959.

75   FRANCE. Paris. Pablo Picasso
at the inauguration of one of his murals
at the UNESCO building. 1958.

76   FRANCE. Paris.
Sculptor Alberto Giacometti
in his studio. 1958.

77   FRANCE. Paris.
Studio of Alberto Giacometti. 1958.

78   FRANCE. Paris.
Alberto Giacometti in his studio. 1958.

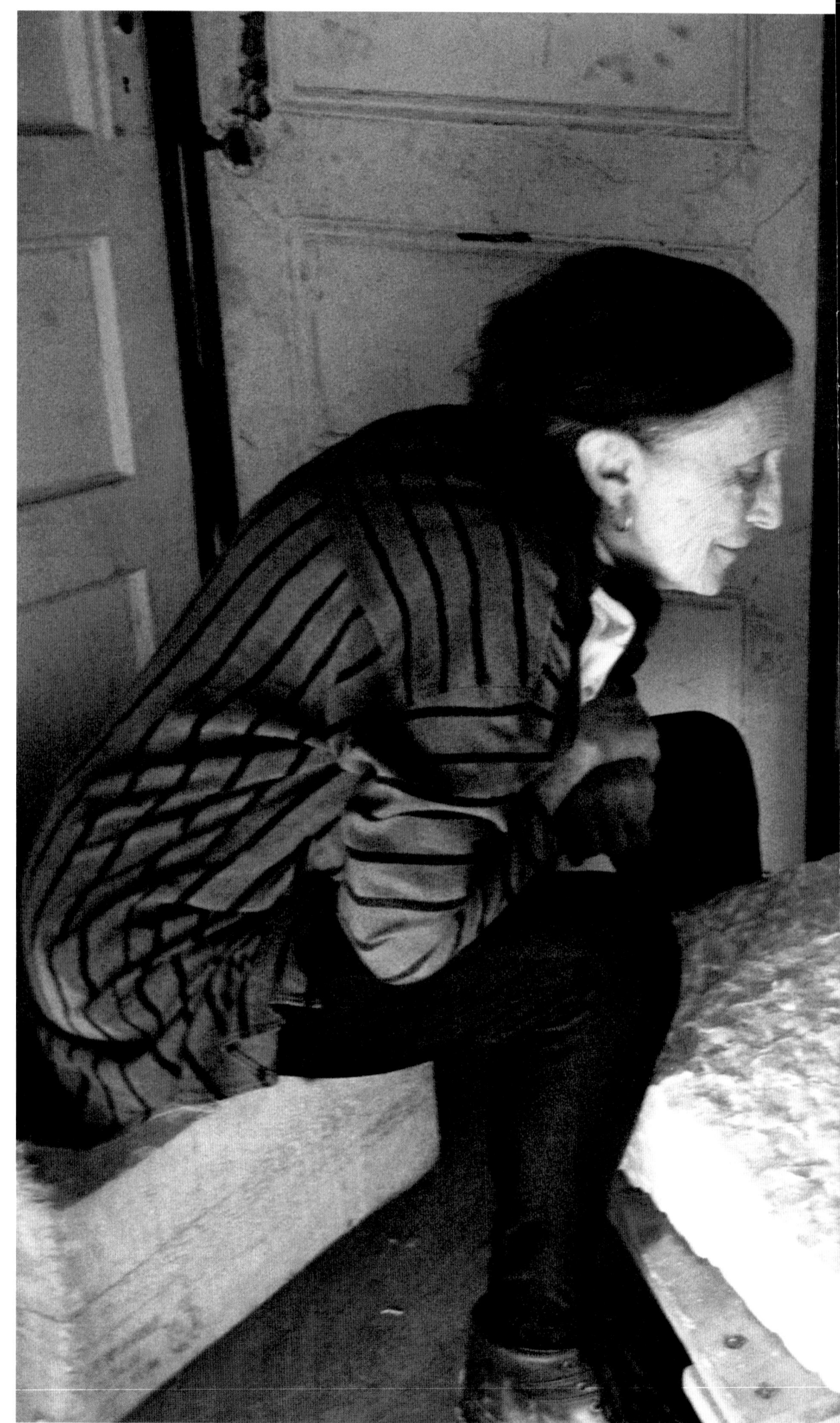

79　USA. Brooklyn, NY.
Louise Bourgeois with her sculpture
To Fall on Deaf Ears. 1991.

80   USA. New York, NY.
Louise Bourgeois and Andy Warhol. 1987.

81   USA. New York, NY.
Louise Bourgeois. 1992.

82 USA. Roxbury, CT.
Alexander Calder. 1966.

83 USA. Roxbury, CT.
Alexander Calder's studio. 1963.

84   USA. Roxbury, CT.
Alexander Calder in his studio. 1963.

Pages 126–127:
85   USA. Roxbury, CT.
Playwright Arthur Miller and artist
Alexander Calder. 1963.

86   USA. New York, NY.
Alex Katz in his studio. 1995.

87   ENGLAND.
Henry Moore in his studio. 1954.

88   USA. New York, NY.
Roy Lichtenstein in his studio. 1997.

89   USA. New York, NY.
Tom Wesselman in his studio. 1995.

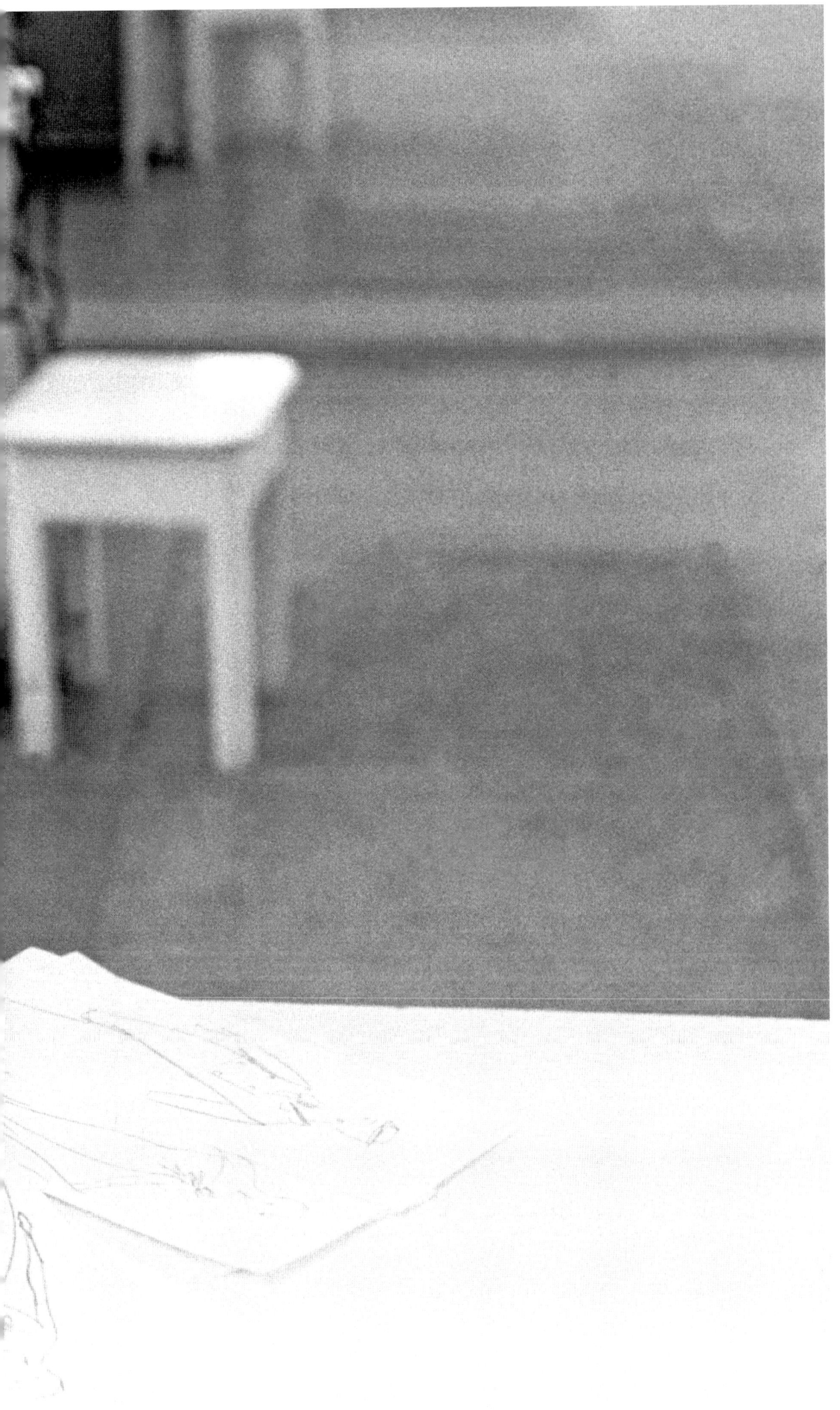

90   FRANCE. Paris.
Yves Saint Laurent preparing
his first fashion show at Dior. 1957.

91 FRANCE. Paris.
Sammy Davis Jr. 1964.

92–93   FRANCE. Paris. French actors
Simone Signoret and Yves Montand. 1959.

94   FRANCE. Paris.
Actress and singer Juliette Greco. 1953.

95   USA. Hollywood, CA.
Actor Charlton Heston. 1959.

96   USA. Roxbury, CT.
Playwright Arthur Miller with
his daughter Rebecca. 1995.

97   USA. Hog Island, MA.
Arthur Miller with daughter Rebecca,
on the set of *The Crucible*. 1995.

98 USA. New York, NY. Filmmaker and
novelist Rebecca Miller. 1995.

99   USA. Reno, NV. Director John
Huston and screenwriter Arthur Miller
during the filming of *The Misfits*. 1960.

Pages 150–151:
100   MEXICO. Durango.
Actress Audrey Hepburn with
her dog Mr Famous. 1959.

101   MEXICO. Durango.
Location shooting for *The Unforgiven*,
directed by John Huston. 1959.

102   MEXICO. Durango.
Actress Audrey Hepburn during the
filming of *The Unforgiven*. 1959.

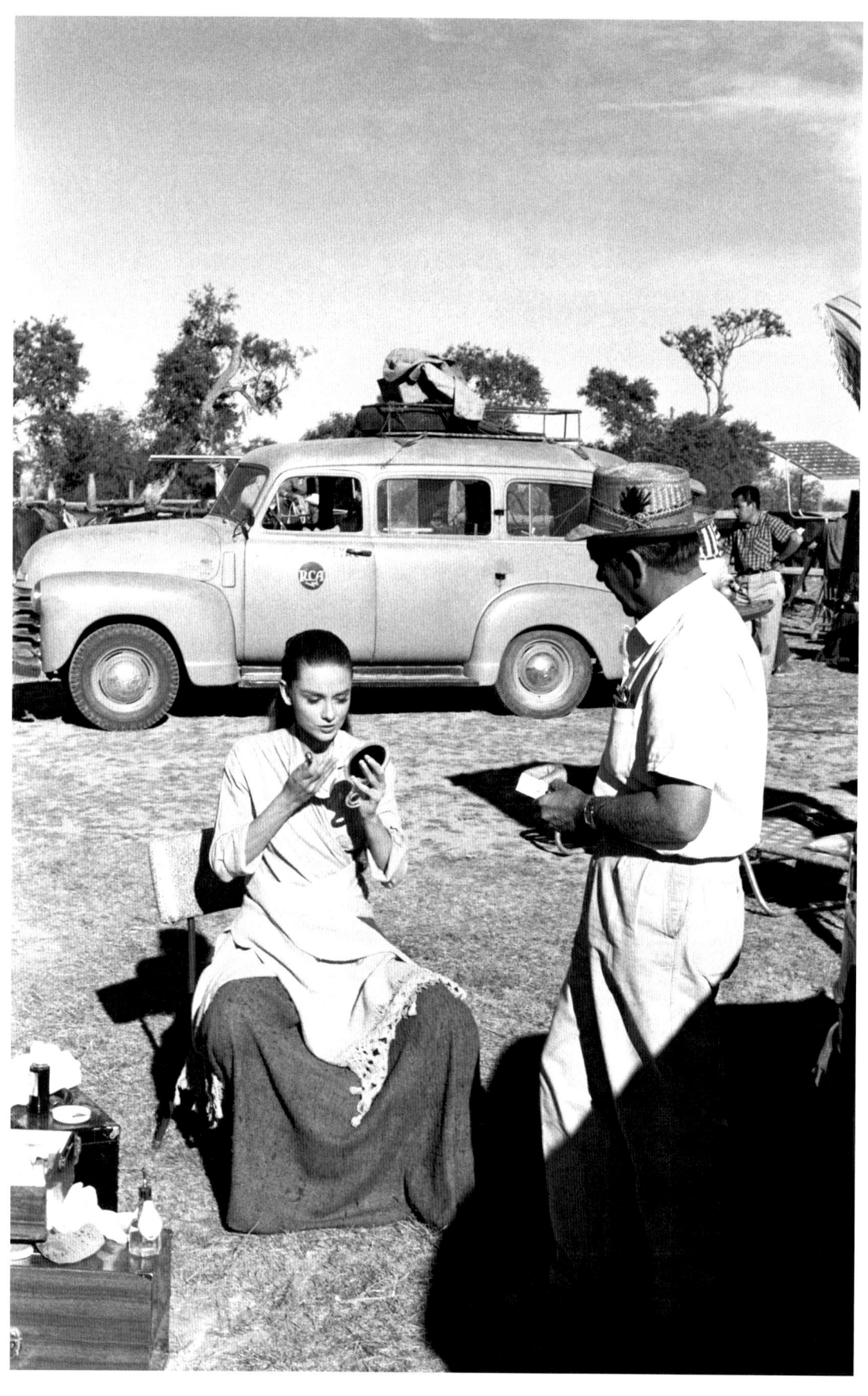

103 MEXICO. Durango.
Audrey Hepburn during the filming
of *The Unforgiven*. 1959.

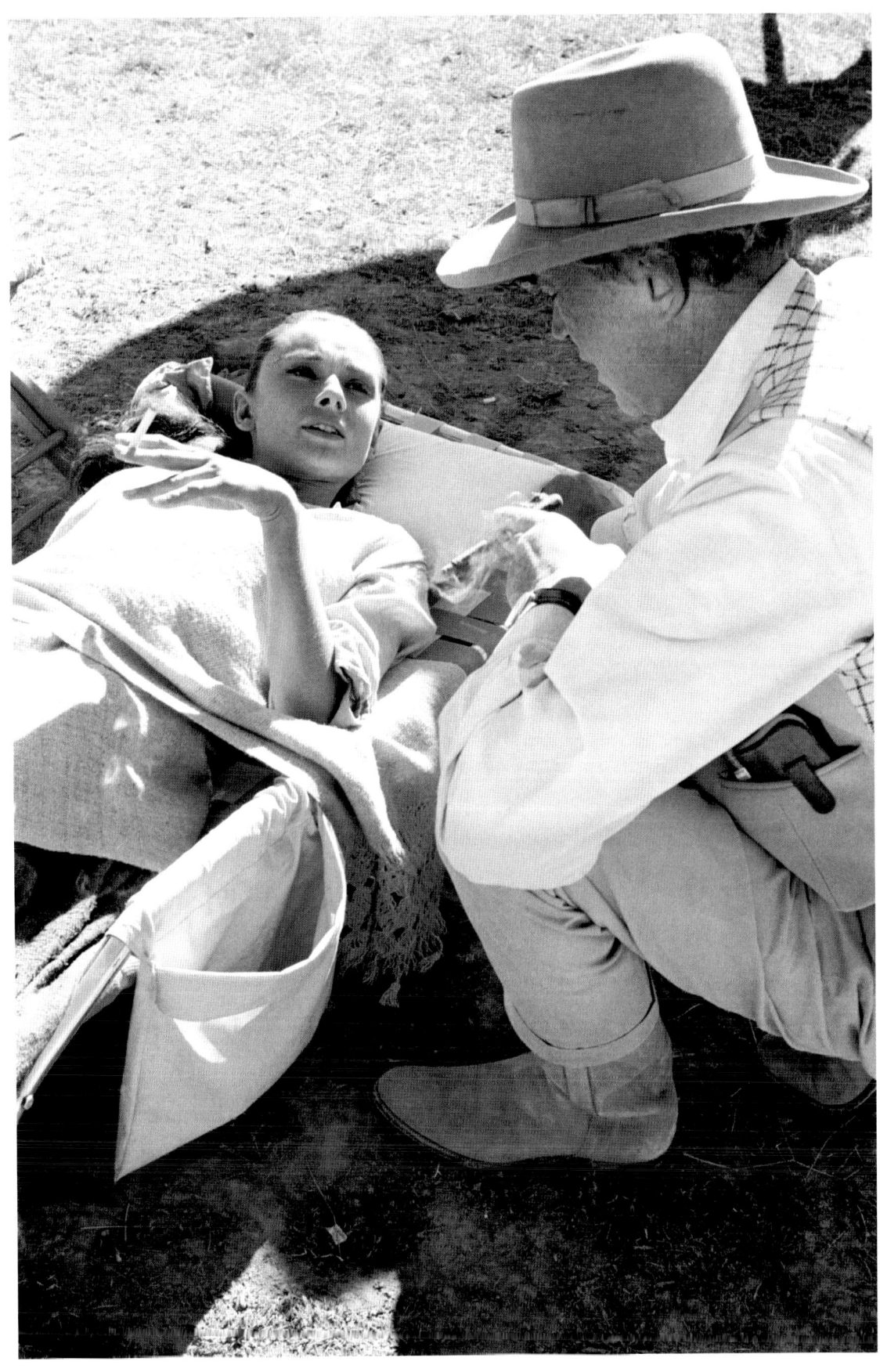

104   MEXICO. Durango. John Huston
and Audrey Hepburn during the filming
of *The Unforgiven*. 1959

105 MEXICO. Durango.
Audrey Hepburn. 1959.

106   FRANCE. Paris.
Actors Ingrid Bergman and Anthony
Perkins on the set of *Goodbye Again*,
directed by Anatole Litvak. 1960.

107   FRANCE. Paris.
Actors Anthony Perkins, Ingrid
Bergman, and Yves Montand
on the set of *Goodbye Again*. 1960.

108   FRANCE. Paris.
Anthony Perkins and Yves Montand
on the set of *Goodbye Again*. 1960.

109   FRANCE. Paris.
Ingrid Bergman and Yves Montand
on the set of *Goodbye Again*. 1960.

110   FRANCE. Paris.
Anthony Perkins and Ingrid Bergman
on the set of *Goodbye Again*. 1960.

111   FRANCE. Paris. French writer
Françoise Sagan with Ingrid Bergman
and Yves Montand. 1960.

112   FRANCE. Paris. Anatole Litvak,
Anthony Perkins, Ingrid Bergman,
and Yves Montand. 1960.

113   FRANCE. Paris. Ingrid Bergman
on the set of *Goodbye Again*. 1960.

114   USA. New York, NY. Arthur Miller's
Death of a Salesman on Broadway,
directed by Michael Rudman. John
Malkovich, Kate Reid, Dustin Hoffman,
and Steven Lang. 1984.

115 USA. New York, NY.
Dustin Hoffman and director
Volker Schloendorff on the film set
of *Death of a Salesman*. 1985.

116   ENGLAND. Actor José Ferrer
as Toulouse Lautrec, with
director John Huston on the set
of *Moulin Rouge*. 1953.

117   ENGLAND. Actress Zsa Zsa Gabor
during the filming of *Moulin Rouge*. 1953.

118–120   SPAIN. Madrid.
Actress Gina Lollobrigida on the set
of *Solomon and Sheba*, directed by
King Vidor. 1958.

121　ARGENTINA. Salta.
Actress Christine Kaufmann
on the set of *Taras Bulba*,
directed by J. Lee Thompson. 1961.

122–123 ARGENTINA. Salta.
Christine Kaufmann. 1961.

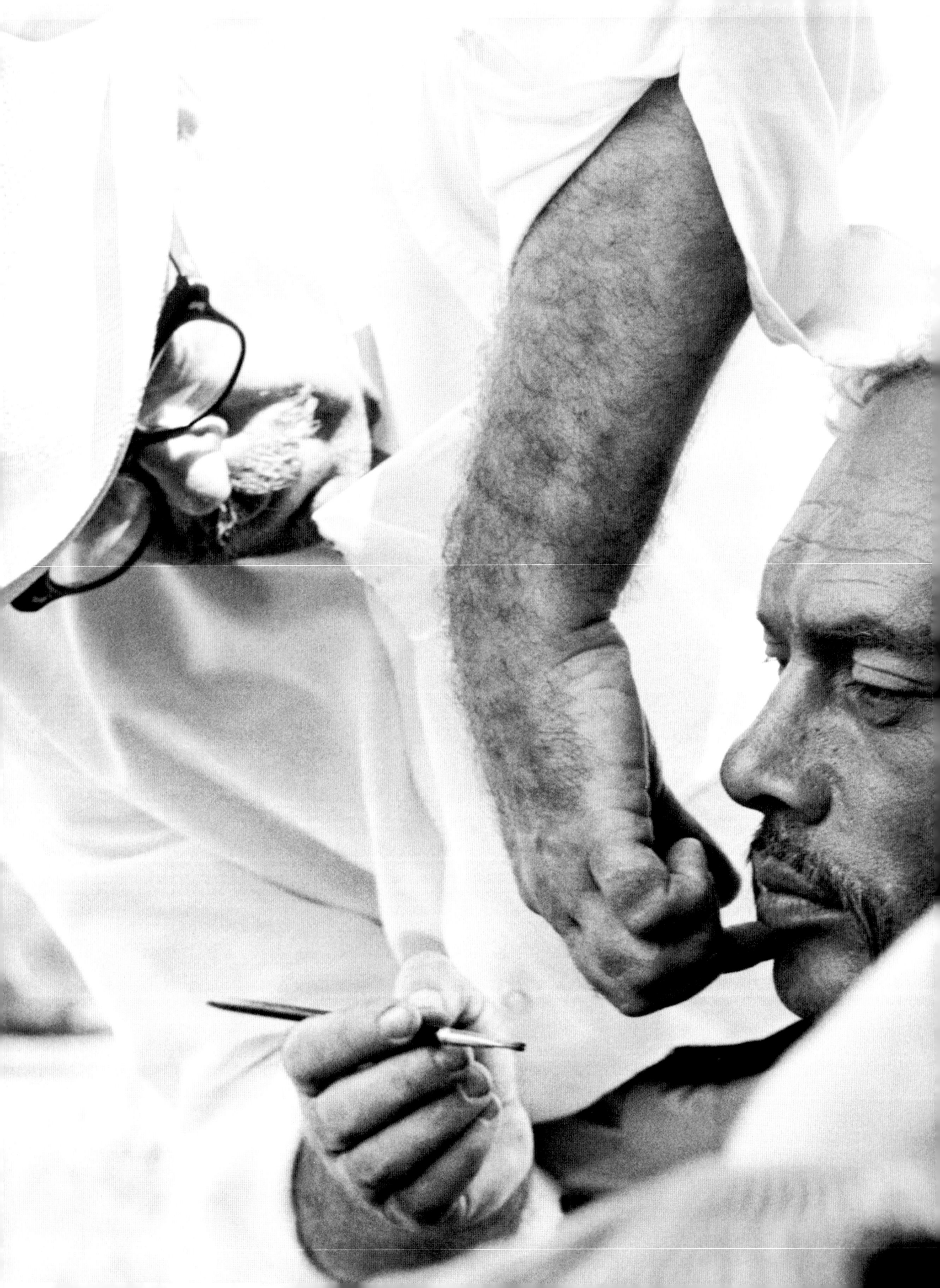

Pages 176–177:
124   ARGENTINA. Salta. Actors
Yul Brynner and Christine Kaufmann
during a makeup session on the set
of *Taras Bulba*. 1961.

125–126   ARGENTINA. Salta.
Yul Brynner on the set of *Taras Bulba*. 1961.

127   ARGENTINA. Salta.
Inge Morath on the set of *Taras Bulba*.
Photographer unknown. 1961.

128   ARGENTINA. Salta.
Actor Tony Curtis on the set
of *Taras Bulba*. 1961.

129 USA. Reno, NV. Playwright Arthur Miller and director John Huston during the filming of *The Misfits*. 1960.

130   USA. Reno, NV.
Actor Clark Gable during the
filming of *The Misfits*. 1960.

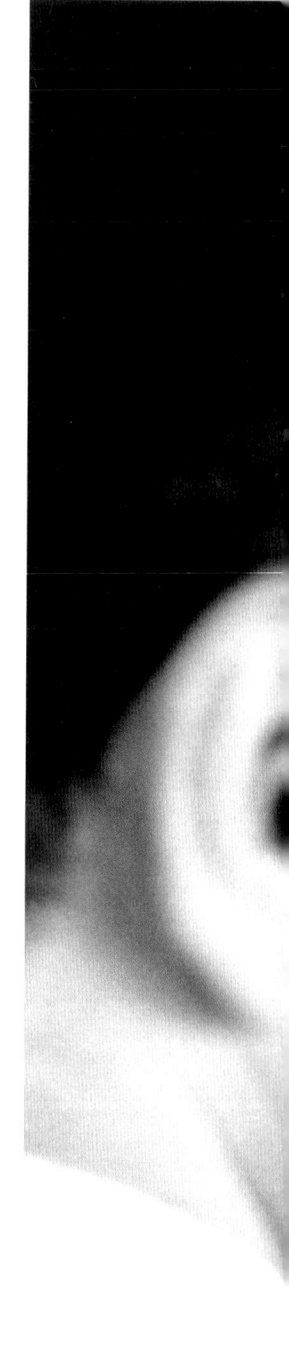

131   USA. Reno, NV. Actors Marilyn
Monroe and Eli Wallach rehearsing
during the filming of *The Misfits*. 1960.

132   USA. Reno, NV. Clark Gable
and Marilyn Monroe on the set
of *The Misfits*. 1960.

133　USA. Reno, NV. John Huston,
Marilyn Monroe, and Arthur Miller on
the set of *The Misfits*. 1960.

134–139 USA. Reno, NV.
Marilyn Monroe and Eli Wallach
rehearsing a dance scene during
the filming of *The Misfits*. 1960.

140   USA. Reno, NV. Clark Gable during
the filming of *The Misfits*. 1960.

141   USA. Reno, NV. Marilyn Monroe
during the filming of *The Misfits*. 1960.

USA. Reno, NV. Marilyn Monroe
and Arthur Miller after a day's
shooting of *The Misfits*. 1960.

143–144   USA. Reno, NV.
Marilyn Monroe on the set
of *The Misfits*. 1960.

145   USA. Reno, NV. 1960.

146   USA. Reno, NV. 1960.

147–148 USA. Reno, NV. 1960.

FRANCE, SPAIN
RUSSIA, IRAN, CHINA

149   FRANCE. Paris.
Place de Furstemberg. 1958.

150   FRANCE. Paris.
Before the auction at Drouot. 1954.

151   FRANCE. Enghien-les-Bains. 1954.

152   FRANCE. Paris. 1953.

153   FRANCE. Paris. 1955.

154   FRANCE. Paris. 1958.

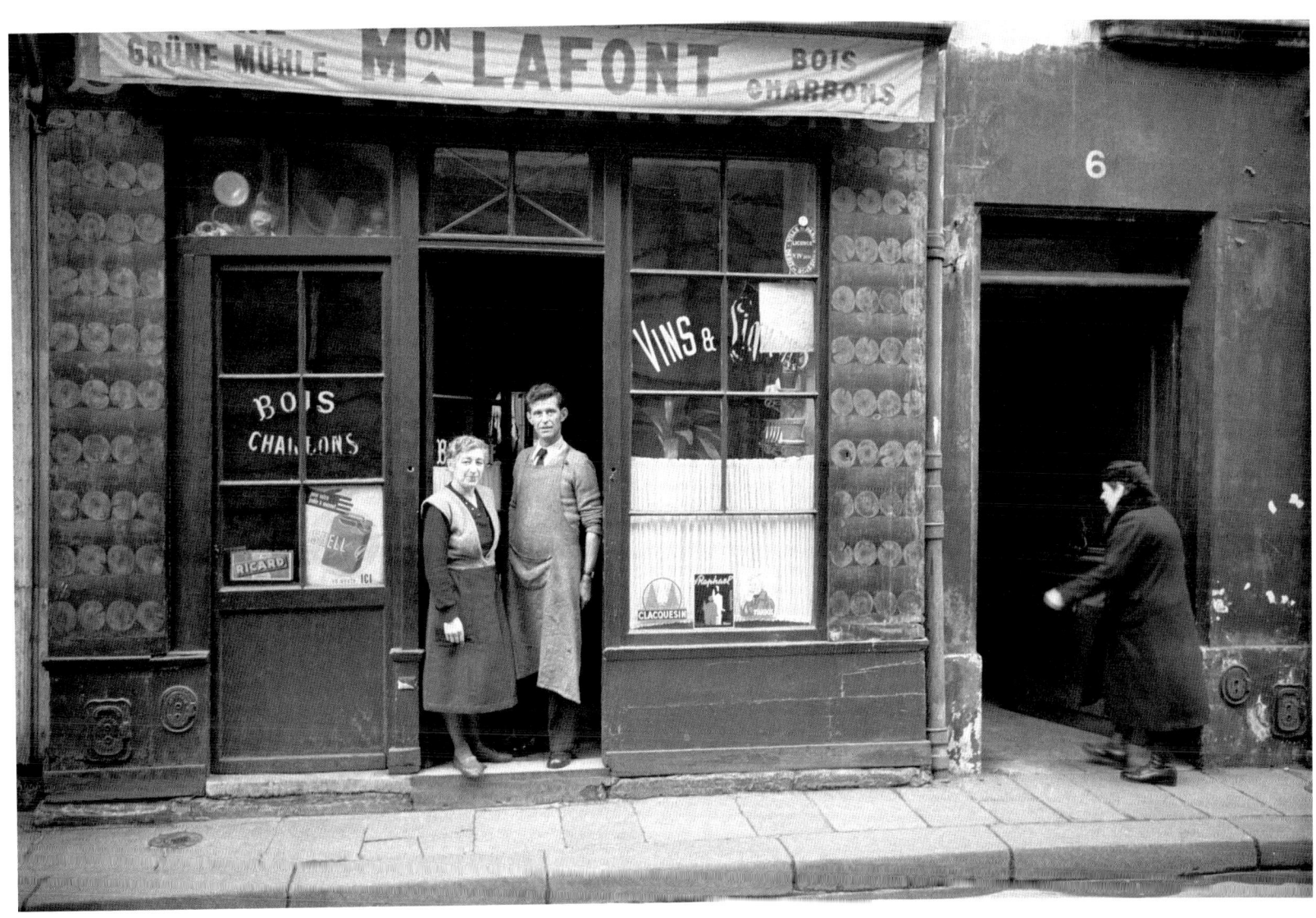

155 FRANCE. Paris. 1955.   156–157 FRANCE. Paris. 1956.

158   FRANCE. Paris. 1958.

159   SPAIN. Madrid. Mercedes Fórmica,
lawyer and writer. 1955.

160 SPAIN. Madrid.
Calle Mayor, Sunday afternoon. 1992.

161 SPAIN. Pamplona.
During the festival of San Fermin. 1954.

162–163 SPAIN. Pamplona.
During the festival of San Fermin. 1954.

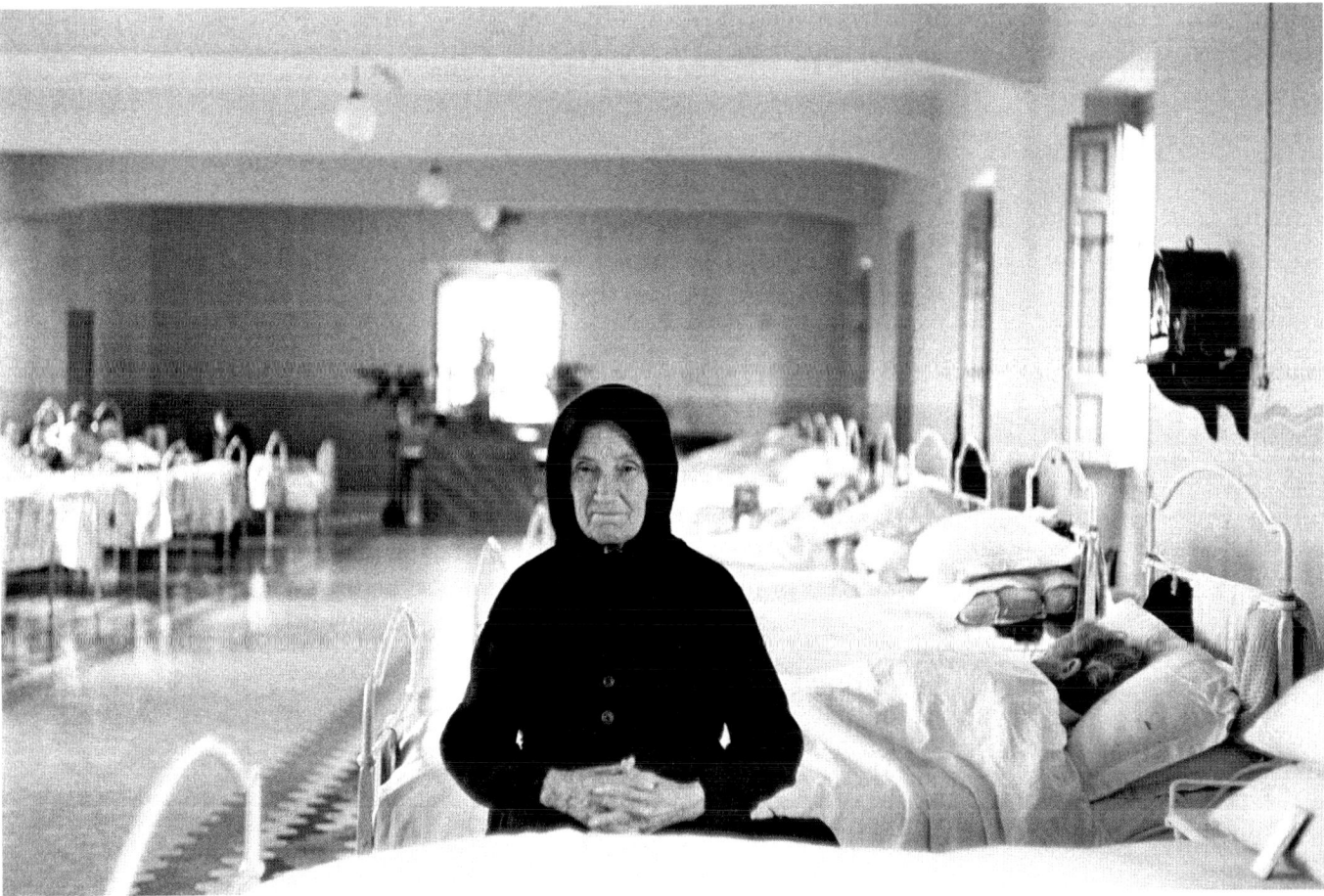

164　SPAIN. Pamplona. 1954.

165　SPAIN. Toledo.
Street behind cathedral. 1961.

166　SPAIN. Pamplona.
During the festival of San Fermin
hospital beds are ready
for possible casualties. 1954.

167   SPAIN. La Alberca.
Late Sunday afternoon on
the main village square. 1955.

168   SPAIN. Cordoba.
In a village cafe. 1962.

169–170   SPAIN. Pamplona.
During the festival of San Fermin. 1954.

171   SPAIN. Pamplona.
During the festival of San Fermin. 1954.

172–173   SPAIN. Pamplona.
During the festival of San Fermin. 1954.

174   SPAIN. Pamplona.
Horse market. 1954.

175   SPAIN. Almonte, Andalusia.
Romeria del Rocio. Siesta of the
oxen driver. 1955.

176   SPAIN. Pamplona. 1954.

177 SPAIN. Pamplona.
Fiesta of San Fermin.
Couple looking at Corrida. 1954.

178 SPAIN. Pamplona.
Fiesta of San Fermin. Spectators
looking at Corrida. 1954.

179 SPAIN. Pamplona.
During the festival of San Fermin.
Amateurs are allowed in the arena. 1954.

180   SPAIN. Madrid.
Entrance of the Picadors at the
beginning of the Corrida. Plaza de Toros
during the Feria de San Isidro. 1955.

181   SPAIN. Pamplona.
Luis Miguel Dominguin. 1957.

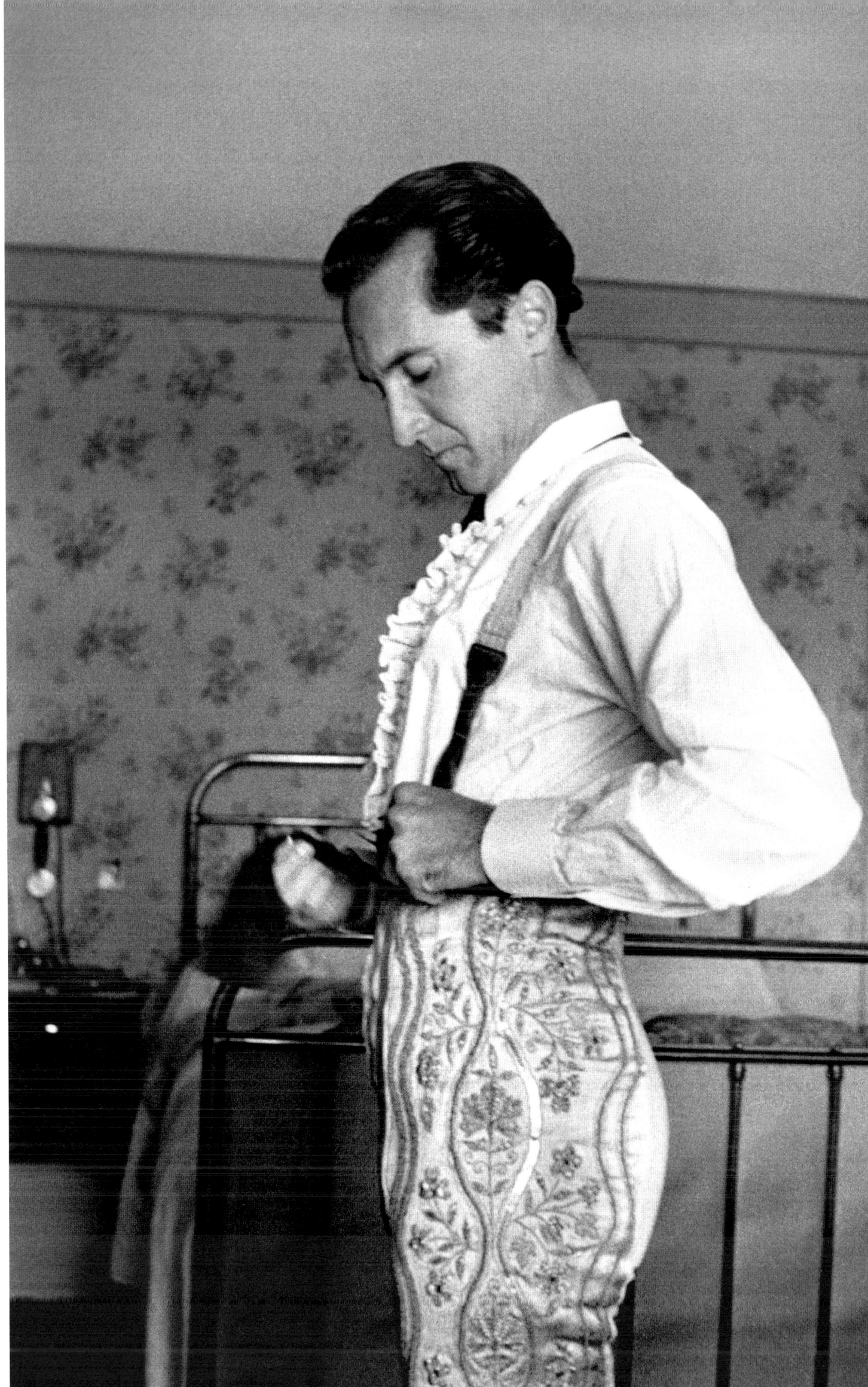

182   SPAIN. Pamplona. Fiesta of San
Fermin. The torero César Girón. 1954.

Pages 244-245:
183   USSR. Leningrad. Writer
Joseph Brodsky on the roof of the
Peter and Paul Fortress, a former
Czarist prison. 1967.

184   USSR. Moscow.
Red Square. Line of people
queuing up all day to go through
the Lenin Mausoleum. 1965.

185   USSR. Zagorsk Monastery.
Sunday Mass. 1988.

186   USSR. Pereslavl Zalessky.
Abandoned monastery. 1967.

187 USSR. Leningrad.
Courtyard between Raskolnikov's
lodgings and pawnbroker's flat,
as described in Fyodor Dostoyevsky's
Crime and Punishment. 1967.

188 USSR. Moscow.
Little girl expecting her
parents' guests. 1989.

189   USSR. Train Lomonosov –
Leningrad. Couple returning from
Dacha with bags of food. 1989.

190   USSR. Leningrad.
Scene taken from inside
Winter Palace. 1965.

191   USSR. Moscow.
Prima ballerina Maya Plisetskaya
at the Bolshoi Theater. 1967.

192   IRAN. Qum. Inge Morath.
Photographer unknown. 1956.

Pages 256–257:
193   IRAN. Persepolis.
Columns of the Apadana. 1956.

194   IRAN. Isfahan. View of the
Maidan-i-Shah, the main square
of Isfahan. 1956.

195–196   IRAN. Yazd. 1956.

197   IRAN. Research laboratory
at the Abadan refinery. 1956.

198   IRAN. Abadan. English and Iranian
technicians during nightshift in the control room of the Catalytic Cracker. 1956.

199   IRAN. Industrial suburbs of Tehran
with brick factories. Snow capped
Alborz mountains in the distance. 1956.

200   CHINA. Beijing.
Actress in Arthur Miller's play
Death of a Salesman at the Beijing
People's Art Theater. 1983.

201   CHINA. Beijing.
Rehearsing the fight scene in the
Beijing production of Arthur Miller's
play *Death of a Salesman*. 1983.

202   CHINA. Beijing.
Rehearsing *Death of a Salesman*
at the People's Art Theater. 1983.

203   CHINA. Beijing. Arthur Miller, lead
actor Ying Ruocheng and cast during
the Beijing production of *Death of a
Salesman*. 1983.

204   CHINA. Beijing. Arthur Miller
during a visit to the Capitol Theater.
On Miller's right is China's best known
playwright Cao Yu. 1978.

205   CHINA. Beijing.
Rehearsing *Death of a Salesman* at the
People's Art Theater. Arthur Miller and
Ying Ruocheng. 1983

206   CHINA. Beijing. Rehearsing
Death of a Salesman at the People's Art
Theater. Arthur Miller. 1983.

207   CHINA. Beijing.
Death of a Salesman at the People's Art
Theater. Ying Ruocheng (left). 1983.

208   CHINA. Beijing.
Death of a Salesman at the People's
Art Theater. Arthur Miller (center),
Ying Ruocheng (seated, right). 1983.

209   CHINA. Soldiers on Yuan Dynasty
sculpture of a Maitreya. West Lake near
Hangzhou. 1978.

210   CHINA. Hangzhou.
Arthur Miller with his
interpreter, Su Guang. 1978.

Our special thanks to Rebecca Miller
for trusting us to honor her mother's legacy.

BIOGRAPHY INGE MORATH

Photography is a strange phenomenon. In spite of the use of that technical instrument, the camera, no two photographers, even if they were at the same place at the same time, come back with the same pictures. The personal vision is usually there from the beginning; result of a special chemistry of background and feelings, traditions and their rejection, of sensibility and voyeurism. You trust your eye and you cannot help but bear your soul. One's vision finds of necessity the form suitable to express it.—Inge Morath

(*Inge Morath: Life as a Photographer*, Kehayoff Verlag, 1999)

Inge Morath (1923–2002) was born in Graz, Austria. Her parents were scientists whose work took them to different laboratories and universities in Europe during her childhood. Educated in French-speaking schools, Morath and her family relocated to Darmstadt in the 1930s, and then to Berlin.

Morath's first encounter with avant-garde art was at the *Entartete Kunst* ("Degenerate Art") exhibition organized by the Nazi party in 1937, which sought to inflame public opinion against modern art. "I found a number of these paintings exciting and fell in love with Franz Marc's *Blue Horse*," Morath later wrote. "Only negative comments were allowed, and thus began a long period of keeping silent and concealing thoughts."

After the Second World War, Morath worked as a translator and journalist. In 1948, she was hired by Warren Trabant for *Heute*, an illustrated magazine published by the US Information Agency in Munich. Morath had encountered photographer Ernst Haas in Vienna and brought his work to Trabant's attention. Working together for *Heute*, Morath wrote articles to accompany Haas' pictures. In 1949, Morath and Haas were invited by Robert Capa to join the newly-founded Magnum Photos in Paris, where she would work as an editor. Working with contact sheets by founding member Henri Cartier-Bresson fascinated Morath. She wrote, "I think that in studying his way of photographing I learned how to photograph myself before I ever took a camera into my hand."

Morath was briefly married to the British journalist Lionel Birch and relocated to London in 1951. That same year, she began to photograph during a visit to Venice. "It was instantly clear to me that from now on I would be a photographer," she wrote. "As I continued to photograph I became quite joyous. I knew that I could express the things I wanted to say by giving them form through my eyes." Morath divorced Birch and returned to Paris to pursue a career in photography.

In 1955 she was invited to become a full member of Magnum Photos. During the late 1950s, she travelled widely, covering stories in Europe, the Middle East, Africa, the United States, and South America for such publications as *Holiday*, *Paris Match*, and *Vogue*. She published *Guerre à la Tristesse*, photographs of Spain, with Robert Delpire in 1955, followed by *De la Perse à l'Iran*, photographs of Iran, in 1958.

Like many Magnum members, Morath worked as a still photographer on numerous motion picture sets. Having met director John Huston while she was living in London, Morath worked on several of his films. In 1960 she was on the set of *The Misfits*, a blockbuster film featuring Marilyn Monroe, Clark Gable, and Montgomery Clift, with a screenplay by Arthur Miller. Morath met Miller while working on *The Misfits*, and— following Miller's divorce from Monroe—they were married on February 17, 1962.

Morath's achievements during her first decade of work as a photographer are significant. Along with Eve Arnold, she was among the first women members of Magnum Photos, which remains to this day a predominantly male organization. Many critics have written of the element of playful surrealism that characterizes Morath's work from this period. It was motivated by a fundamental humanism, shaped as much by the experience of war as by its lingering shadow over post-war Europe. This motivation grows, in Morath's mature work, into a motif as she documents the endurance of the human spirit under situations of extreme duress as well as its manifestations of ecstasy and joy.

Ingeborg Morath Miller died of cancer in 2002, at the age of 78. In honour of their colleague, the members of Magnum Photos established the Inge Morath Award in 2002. The Award is administered by the Inge Morath Foundation in cooperation with the Magnum Foundation, New York. The Inge Morath archive was acquired by the Beinecke Library at Yale University in 2014, and the material is open for research

VORWORT

Für mich als Kind war meine Mutter eine schwer zu
fassende und faszinierende Person. Sie war sehr eigen,
tief emotional, bescheiden, elegant und sehr großzügig.
Sie war verwundet. Sie war furchtlos. Sie war mit wilder
Entschlossenheit Mutter. Und sie war eine enorme
Künstlerin.

Als Heranwachsende sah ich in Inge eine Frau, die aus
einer grauenvollen, mythischen Vergangenheit kam.
Sie war in einem Kessel des abgrundtief Bösen ge-
schmiedet worden, hatte im heißesten Teil der Hölle –
Nazi-Deutschland – gelebt und trug lebenslange, innere
Narben davon, in den Bauch des Ungeheuers geblickt
zu haben. Eine Begebenheit aus dieser Zeit scheint mir
jedoch am meisten über ihren Charakter zu erzählen.
Im Jahr 1945, mit zweiundzwanzig, sie lebte allein in
Berlin, um ihr Studium abzuschließen, während ihre
Eltern in Salzburg arbeiteten, leistete sie sich einen
kleinen Veilchenstrauß, den sie einer alten Frau auf der
Straße abkaufte. In diesem Moment ertönte Flieger-
alarm. Inge hörte die Bomber näherkommen und rannte
mit anderen verzweifelten Menschen zu einem Luft-
schutzbunker. Überzeugt, dass bald Bomben auf sie
niederregnen würden, hielt sie sich schützend den Veilchenstrauß über den Kopf. Als sie in Sicherheit war,
merkte sie, wie albern dieser Instinkt gewesen war.
Aber in dieser Geste offenbarte sich ihr Wesen. Inge
glaubte an die Schönheit. Schönheit war für sie eine Art
Religion. Sie murmelte oft „beauté, mon beau désir …".
Vielleicht wandte sie, die als junge Frau so viel Häss-
liches miterlebt hatte, sich der Schönheit zu, insbeson-
dere der Schönheit der Kunst als Zeichen dafür, dass
menschliche Wesen noch immer fähig waren, etwas
Unversehrtes zu erschaffen, etwas Schönes und damit
Gutes. Als Photographin war sie von Künstlern fasziniert;
ihre verführerische, lebhafte Art ließ deren Schutzpan-
zer dahinschmelzen. Sie verstand die Anforderungen
großer, fragiler Egos. Doch was ihr gesamtes Werk –
von Portraits berühmter Schriftsteller und Schauspieler
bis zu den Bildern von Frauen auf den Straßen des Iran
oder schachspielenden Senioren im Park – verbindet,
ist ein ausgeprägter Sinn für Geometrie. Die Bilder sind
von einem am lebenslangen Studium großer Kunst ge-
schärften Instinkt schön komponiert. Inge war von ihrer
Mutter, einer Wissenschaftlerin, als Kind in die Nazi-
Ausstellung „Entartete Kunst" mitgenommen worden
und war schon früh überzeugt, dass Kunst keineswegs
frivol oder dekadent, sondern essenziell ist und oft den
letzten Funken Hoffnung enthält.

Ich habe erst als Erwachsene erkannt, dass Inge mich
zu einer bildenden Künstlerin erziehen wollte. Sie
besuchte mit mir Museen, um Gemälde zu betrachten,
blätterte mit mir in Photobüchern, analysierte gelegent-
lich ihre eigenen, erfolgreicheren Bilder – ließ mich den
Goldenen Schnitt suchen und die Wirkung des Dreiecks
verstehen, die beinahe mystische Geometrie, die ein
Bild stärker verankert als Stimmung oder Sujet – all
das wurde, ohne großes Trara, in meinen kleinen Kopf
geschleust. Als Mutter hielt Inge nichts von Regeln oder
Strafe; sie lehrte durch ihr Vorbild. Ihre Selbstdisziplin
war legendär. Sie lernte gut genug Russisch und
Chinesisch, um in beiden Sprachen Dichtung lesen und
sich unterhalten zu können, bevor sie versuchte, in diese Kulturen als Photographin einzudringen. Wenn sie ein
Nickerchen hielt, dann auf dem blanken Linoleumboden
ihres Studios, umgeben von ihren geliebten Schäfer-
hunden, die sie dösend bewachten.

Worte können das komplexe, mysteriöse Rätsel von
Inge Moraths Persönlichkeit nicht lösen. Aber wir haben
ihre Photographien, sie erzählen von ihrer Empathie,
ihrem mangelnden Narzissmus, ihrer Neugierde auf
andere menschliche Wesen und Kulturen, von ihrer
Hoffnung, die Kunst könne eine Kerze gegen die dunk-
leren Elemente der menschlichen Natur sein.

Rebecca Miller

INGE MORATH
ICH TRAUE MEINEN AUGEN

Meine Damen und Herren,

Ich bin in Berlin während des Zweiten Weltkriegs in die Schule und später auf die Universität gegangen. Es war eine schwierige Zeit, es war ein Teil meiner Jugend, die Erinnerungen sind kunterbunt und vielschichtig, verwaschen und scharf. Was ich hier versuchen will, ist, den Erlebnissen und Ereignissen nachzugehen, die mich zu einer Person machten, die ihren Augen traut und letzten Endes Photographin wurde, ein Beruf, von dem ich nicht nur nie träumte, sondern von dessen Existenz ich kaum etwas wusste. Ich bin gebürtige Österreicherin. Meine Eltern waren Wissenschaftler, arbeiteten in verschiedenen Laboratorien und Universitäten. Wir zogen daher oft um, wechselten je nach Wohnort Schulen und Sprachen: Mein erstes Schuljahr verbrachte ich in einer von Nonnen geführten Dorfschule in Frankreich. Da meine Eltern dieses Wanderleben nicht ungewöhnlich fanden, fiel es meinem um ein Jahr jüngeren Bruder und mir kaum auf.

Es gab in der Familie zwei Photoapparate: Einer gehörte meiner Mutter, eine Contax, die im chemischen Laboratorium meines Vaters, mit dem sie zusammenarbeitete, auf ein Mikroskop geschraubt war. Damit photographierte sie Zellstrukturen, die sie für wissenschaftliche Zwecke, aber mit einem gewissen künstlerischen Flair einfärbte. Mein Vater benutzte die Diapositive für seine Vorträge. Es waren abstrakte Photos, die mir gefielen, aber, da ich keine besonderen wissenschaftlichen Neigungen hatte, mich nicht berührten. Die andere Kamera war ein großformatiger Kasten und gehörte meinem Großvater. Dazu hatte er ein Stativ und ein schwarzes Tuch, unter das er auf längere Zeit verschwand, während mein Bruder oder ich, berstend vor Ungeduld, für sein Photo dekorativ auf Brunnenrändern hockten, bis endlich der erlösende Klick zu hören war.

Wenn ich damals einige Objektivität besessen hätte, hätte ich zugeben müssen, dass die Behandlung des Lichtes auf diesen Photos sehr schön war. Jedoch schien mir der festgehaltene Moment ohne Interesse: Da war ich und saß auf einem Brunnenrand, der nichts mit mir zu tun hatte. Da war weder Überraschendes noch Geheimnisvolles, wie es mich aus den Illustrationen der aus der elterlichen Bibliothek geborgten Bücher ansprang.

Gemälde wirkten auf mich mit der gleichen Anziehungskraft des nicht ganz Erklärlichen, selbst in konventioneller Form. Ich sah sie mir überall an, in Warte- und Wohnzimmern und in den Schlafzimmern meiner Großeltern, Tanten und Onkel, in denen Reproduktionen von Böcklin und Feuerbach enigmatisch auf meine Einbildungskraft wirkten. Meine Mutter liebte Dürer und Barockes. Natürlich besuchten wir Museen. Aber ich kann mich nicht an moderne oder Avantgarde-Werke erinnern.

Ich hatte jedoch meine eigene Begegnung mit der Moderne. Vor dem Umzug nach Berlin wohnten wir eine Zeitlang in Darmstadt, in einer Wohnung, die nur ein paar Minuten von einem Hügel namens Mathildenhöhe entfernt lag. Dort gab es eine von dem Großherzog von Hessen gegründete Künstlerkolonie, deren Bauten fast ausschließlich von dem Architekten Joseph Maria Olbrich entworfen waren. Er schuf in seiner eigenwilligen, vom Jugendstil inspirierten Bauweise ein erstaunliches Ensemble von Häusern, Gärten, großen Atelierbauten und einem fünffingrigen Turm, der gleichzeitig die Landschaft dominierte und eine großherzogliche Hochzeit feierte.

Eine ältere, ebenfalls mit einem großherzoglichen Ereignis verbundene Russische Kapelle stand in der Nähe in bizarrem Kontrast zu den klaren Linien der Jugendstilbauten. Mysteriöse Reliefs auf denen, soweit ich mich erinnere, nackte Frauen Musikinstrumente spielten, tauchten hier und da im Dunkel eines unter dem Turm liegenden Platanenhains auf; die gefleckten Stämme der Bäume schienen ein eigenes Leben zu führen.

Die Begegnung mit der Mathildenhöhe war mein erstes wichtiges visuelles Erlebnis. Anderes Unvergessenes aus dieser Zeit waren Theaterbesuche, meine erste Oper, *Mignon*, die mich zu Tränen rührte, indische Studenten meines Vaters, die eine Zeitlang bei uns wohnten, ihr exotisches Essen selbst kochten, phantastische Geschichten über ihre Heimat erzählten und uns eher als Barbaren betrachteten, und eine befreundete extravagante Tänzerin, die mit Harald Kreuzberg aufgetreten war und uns eine Sammlung von Grammophonplatten mit Jazzmusik hinterließ. Ziemlich bald zog die neue Ordnung des nun fest etablierten Naziregimes den Vorhang über diese Kindheit zu. Natürlich war mir noch nicht klar, dass fast alles, das ich schön gefunden hatte, in Kürze nicht nur für tabu, sondern für zersetzerisch auf den deutschen Geist wirkend erklärt werden würde.

Gegen Ende der dreißiger Jahre zogen wir nach Berlin, wo mein Vater ein Holzforschungsinstitut leitete; meine Mutter arbeitete wie immer mit ihm als Assistentin. Ich wurde in die Luisenschule geschickt, einen roten

Backsteinbau in der Ziegelstraße, ein paar Schritte vom Bahnhof Friedrichstraße entfernt. Meine Mutter hatte sich in ein Haus mit einem großen Garten in Bergfelde verliebt, was bedeutete, dass wir uns täglich zwei Stunden mit Fahrrad und S-Bahn auf dem Hin- und Rückweg zur beziehungsweise von der Schule befanden. Später zogen wir um nach Wilmersdorf, gerade rechtzeitig für die Bombenangriffe. Die Atmosphäre wurde fühlbar bedrückender: Bücher, die immer in der vorderen Reihe der Bücherschränke gestanden hatten, wanderten nach hinten; die Jazzplatten verschwanden. Man sagte uns, dass Denunziation gefährlich sein könnte, und meine impulsive Mutter, deren Reaktionen eher auf spontanem Gefühl als politischem Denken beruhten, sagte nur noch in kleinem Kreise, wie abscheulich das Braun der SA-Uniformen sei. Das Wort „verboten" nahm neue Dimensionen an, und dann kam das Wort „entartet". Ich persönlich verdanke der 1937 vom Propagandaministerium organisierten Ausstellung „Entartete Kunst" meine erste wichtige Begegnung mit der Avantgarde. Reproduktionen der verpönten Gemälde wurden in Schulkorridoren zur Schau gestellt, um uns die obligaten Hassgefühle einzuflößen. Ich fand viele der Gemälde aufregend und verliebte mich in Franz Marcs *Blaues Pferd*. Meine Technik war es, das Gemälde so lange anzustarren, bis ich es mit geschlossenen Augen in allen Details vor mir sehen konnte.

Nur negative Kommentare wurden gebilligt, und so begann die lange Periode des Schweigens und Verschweigens, aus der ein genaueres Hinsehen geboren und zur Gewohnheit wurde. Gesichter sind offene Bücher, und man begann, sich mit den Augen mitzuteilen, was Münder nicht mehr zu sagen wagten.

An die damaligen Illustrierten kann ich mich kaum erinnern. 1939 rückte näher, Photos dienten der Propaganda, und es interessierte mich überhaupt nicht, sie anzuschauen. Das Dritte Reich hatte die Besetzung des eigenen Landes so gut wie beendet. Was verlangt wurde, war, wenn nicht Begeisterung, dann zumindest blinder Gehorsam.

Der Zweite Weltkrieg brach aus. Das Leben wurde freudloser. Es gab noch kostenlose Brötchen bei Aschinger, wenn man ein Paar Würstl kaufte, Kinos mit Wurlitzer-Orgeln und amerikanischen Filmen, ausgezeichnete Theateraufführungen und Konzerte in Berlin. Aber zu Hause durfte man nicht mehr ausländische Sender abhören, zumindest nur unter einer Decke. Wir machten Kriegsabitur, dann Dienst in einem Kindergarten für Berliner Arbeiterkinder, deren Väter uns „Intellektuellen" mit allem möglichen Handgreiflichen drohten, wenn sich ihre lieben Kleinen über uns beschwerten. Danach kamen sechs Monate Arbeitsdienst, zu dem ich nach Großborken, einem scheußlichen Nest in den Masuren, geschickt wurde. Glücklichere Schulkolleginnen landeten in der Nähe von Berlin. Es schien unmöglich herauszufinden, wo und warum die Würfel, die das Schicksal zumindest für die nächsten paar Monate bestimmten, fielen.

Die erfolgreiche (mit einer guten Führungsnote versehene) Absolvierung des Arbeitsdienstes war Vorbedingung für die Aufnahme in die Universität. Unter den ungefähr fünfzig Mädchen im Lager waren wir nur zwei, die studieren wollten. Das Lagerleben in Großborken war auf Nivellierung und Formung eines nationalsozialistischen Mädchen- oder Frauentyps zugeschnitten. Die Lagerführerin hieß Clemens und hatte einen Riecher für Nicht-Enthusiasten. Sie überprüfte unsere Unterwäsche und ertappte mich in von zu Hause Mitgebrachtem statt der kratzigen Lagerwäsche, was ihr Grund für tägliche Kontrolle gab. Sie maß die Länge der Röcke unserer ungeschlachten Uniformen vom Boden zum Saum und wog uns jede Woche, denn wir sollten nicht abnehmen. Bücherlesen war verpönt. Da ich es nicht lassen konnte, wurde ich regelmäßig dem Latrinenreinigungsdienst zugeteilt, was mich wenig störte, weil man mich da allein ließ.

Wir mussten singen, wenn wir im Morgengrauen zu den Bauern, denen wir zugeteilt waren, auszogen; die waren übrigens von unserer Anwesenheit ebenso wenig begeistert wie wir vom Dienst bei ihnen. Ich saß viele Stunden in einem dunklen Keller, die Falltür im Küchenboden über mir fest zugeklappt, und keimte in Gesellschaft zahlreicher Mäuse alte Kartoffeln ab. Die Bauern fanden es unterhaltend, meinen Arm tief in einen mit Jauche gefüllten Eimer zu stoßen, der an sich nur für die Wurzeln der zu pflanzenden Rüben bestimmt war. Am meisten amüsierte es sie, ein Stadtmädchen beim Reinigen des von einer ärgerlichen Sau bewohnten Schweinestalls zu beobachten. „Denen werden wir's schon zeigen", sagten sie.

Die meisten anderen Mädchen kamen aus der Umgebung, wir zwei Abiturientinnen waren ihnen fremd, daher verdächtig. Unsere Rettung war, dass sie meistens nicht schreiben konnten und unsere Dienste zur Anfertigung ihrer Liebesbriefe benötigten. Das hinderte sie jedoch nicht daran, auf jede irgendwie verdächtige Bemerkung zu lauern, die sie der Clemens hinterbringen und sich damit in gutes Licht setzen konnten. Jene war begierig auf Material, das unsere Aufnahme in die Universität erschwert oder verhindert hätte. Alle Post wurde zensuriert – es wurde so gut wie unmöglich, ein wahres Wort nach Hause zu schreiben. Ich hoffte, meine Mutter würde zwischen den Zeilen lesen. Die Technik des Verschweigens wurde raffinierter, was verschärfte Beobachtungsgabe notwendig machte. Eine uns sympathische Unterführerin wurde entlassen. Aus Protest begleiteten vier oder fünf von uns sie zum Bahnhof. Strafe folgte auf dem Fuß. Der geringste Ausdruck von Nonkonformismus wurde nicht gelitten.

Ich beschreibe das nur kurz, um die kaum noch glaubliche Atmosphäre dieser Zeit heraufzubeschwören, in die meine Entwicklungsjahre fielen.

In Berlin schaffte ich es, trotz meines nicht gerade schmeichelhaften Abschlusszeugnisses vom Arbeitsdienst, mich zu immatrikulieren. Die Berliner ließen sich in oft bewundernswerter Weise nicht alles diktieren. Irgendwann fingen die Bombenangriffe an. Der Krieg forderte die ersten Opfer innerhalb meiner Familie: Meine drei Cousins fielen, einer nach dem anderen, an verschiedenen Fronten. Sie waren die Gespielen meiner Jugend, ich war während der in Österreich verbrachten Ferien abwechselnd in zwei von ihnen verliebt.

Sie waren kaum zwanzig Jahre alt, und ich erinnere mich an ein nächtliches Gespräch mit dem Schönsten von ihnen. Er trug den Amethyst-Ring seiner Verlobten. Wir saßen nach einem Angriff im dunklen Garten, und er sagte, dass manche seiner Kameraden fühlten, sie wüssten nicht mehr, wofür sie kämpften. „Aber sie harren aus, auch wenn der Posten verloren ist", fügte er hinzu. Ich habe ihn nie wieder gesehen; sein Bruder war schon früher an der Westfront gefallen.

Ich studierte, wo ich einen ruhigen Ort fand, in der Universität und in den U-Bahn-Stationen, die als Luftschutzkeller dienten. Der Studentenschaft trat ich nicht bei. Eines Tages, auf der Heimfahrt, beugte sich ein Professor nahe an mein Ohr, sein Name war Pfeffer, und flüsterte: „Wir werden Sie schon noch erwischen." Mein Vater, der Kampfflieger im Ersten Weltkrieg war, wurde in die Luftwaffenreserve eingezogen. Mein Bruder wurde bei einem seiner ersten Einsätze in seinem Bomber von den Engländern abgeschossen und blieb auf der Vermisstenliste, bis die erlösende Nachricht kam, dass er als Kriegsgefangener in einem Lager in Ägypten war. Meine Mutter arbeitete immer noch im Laboratorium. Wir fuhren in die Umgebung, hamsterten Kartoffeln und was immer sonst zu finden war. Jemand hatte uns denunziert, wir wussten nicht, warum, aber die Lebensmittelkarten wurden auf ein paar Wochen entzogen.

Drei sehr verschiedene Bilder aus dieser Zeit stehen mir noch lebhaft vor Augen: Nach einem Bombenangriff, den wir in einer nahen U-Bahn-Station abwarteten, gingen meine Mutter und ich nach Hause. Die Vorderwand unseres Hauses war eingestürzt, hing in Fetzen vor dem aufgebrochenen Haus, die Zimmer offen zur Straße. Im Erdgeschoß auf dem mit Schutt bedeckten Schreibtisch meines Vaters leuchtete rot und unversehrt unser zerbrechlichster Besitz: eine aus Venedig mitgebrachte urnenförmige Vase aus Rubinglas, die wir als Kinder nie anfassen durften, weil sie so fragil war. Es war wie eine Hoffnung. Wir legten uns in die Betten, von denen wir bloß den Schutt abschüttelten, und schliefen, die Nacht war warm.

Das zweite Bild stammt von einer Aufführung von *Faust*, Zweiter Teil. Gustaf Gründgens spielte den Mephisto. Er trug eine eng wie eine zweite Haut über seinen kahlen Schädel gespannte Lederperücke und sprach einen langen Monolog, rückwärts über einem Felsen hängend, die Lippen dunkelrot geschminkt. Das dritte Bild ist das von einem Flugblatt, es war schon gegen Kriegsende: Es war von den Engländern in der Nacht abgeworfen worden und zeigte eine Photographie von Haufen von Schuhen, von Männer-, Frauen- und Kinderschuhen, und darunter stand, dass alle Besitzer dieser Schuhe im Konzentrationslager von Majdanek umgebracht worden waren. Es war diese Photographie, die bestätigte,

dass alles das Geflüsterte, das Unglaubliche über die Gräuel der Konzentrationslager Wirklichkeit war.

Kurz darauf wurde ich zum Fabrikdienst in Tempelhof eingezogen. Ich bekam einen grauen Ausweis, auf dem stand: „bis zum siegreichen Ende des Krieges". Ich arbeitete an einem Fließband und drehte Schrauben. Die Berliner Arbeiterinnen waren hilfreich und teilten ab und zu sogar mal eine Stulle mit mir. Die meisten Nächte verbrachten wir in Luftschutzkellern. In einer Nacht, nach der Entwarnung, explodierte eine Zeitbombe, ein Pferd ging durch, der Wagen, den es zog, rollte über mich, aber nur mein linkes Bein war aufgerissen. Es war ein kleines Wunder, dass ein Auto kam und hielt. Am Steuer war ein Arzt auf dem Heimweg. Er brachte mich zu meiner Behausung und riet mir, Kohlenstaub in die Wunde zu reiben. „Sie wird heilen. Medikamente haben wir keine mehr." Geblieben ist eine schwärzliche Narbe am linken Schienbein.

Die Russen standen schon kurz vor Berlin. Nach einem schweren Bombenangriff, mit ihrem baldigen Einmarschieren und mit allgemeinem Chaos rechnend, ging ich einfach los, in Richtung Österreich. Meine Eltern hatten sich schon längst nach Salzburg abgesetzt. Wer konnte mich schon finden? Ein paar Soldaten, die dabei waren, eine Brücke zur Sprengung vorzubereiten, ließen mich noch drüber; die gefürchtete Kontrolle der Leute, die die Stadt verließen, schien es nicht mehr zu geben. Einer der Soldaten gab mir ein Stück Wurst.

Bald war ich nicht mehr allein. Alles schien auf der Flucht zu sein. Ein paar Züge gingen noch, also suchte man Bahnhöfe. Alle Plattformen waren vollgestopft von Menschen, viele schleppten ihre letzte Habe. Manchmal gelang es mir, mich irgendwo anzuklammern, ein paar Kilometer zu gewinnen, bis tieffliegende Spitfires den Zug mit Schießen zum Stehen brachten und die Passagiere die Flucht ergriffen, sich flach auf die Erde warfen, um den Angriff abzuwarten. Viele Leute kamen aus dem Osten, aber nur selten wurden Worte gewechselt. Selbst hier, im offensichtlichen Untergang des Naziregimes, riet Vorsicht zum Schweigen.

Es gab kein Wasser zum Waschen, kein Wasser zum Trinken, nirgends konnte man seine Notdurft verrichten. Ich wollte mich in einem Fluss ertränken, aber ein Soldat mit einem Bein zog mich vom Geländer und schrie mich an, er komme aus Russland und ich hätte kein Recht, jetzt sei es sowieso schon gleich aus.

Ich habe später nie Kriege photographiert, aber ich habe Arbeiten über Flüchtlinge gemacht. Ich konnte an ihrem Schicksal die entsetzlichen Folgen aller Kriege zeigen, so wie das Bild der Schuhe von Majdanek die Brutalität aller Konzentrationslager symbolisierte. Ich schaffte es bis Salzburg, fand die Eltern, war krank vor Erschöpfung, hörte kaum, dass die Amerikaner einmarschierten und der Krieg zu Ende war. Wir wurden aus Suppenküchen verpflegt und machten die willkommene Bekanntschaft von Peanutbutter, die die im selben Haus einquartierten amerikanischen Soldaten uns schenkten.

Mein Vater fand eine Anzeige in den unter der amerikanischen Besatzung wieder erscheinenden *Salzburger Nachrichten*, laut der Dolmetscher für den Information Services Branch gesucht wurden. Er schickte mich hin, ich musste anfangen, Geld zu verdienen.

So fand ich meinen ersten Job in der Berggasse in Salzburg. Ich lernte, die aus den Staaten gesendeten Informationen nicht nur zu übersetzen, sondern auch in kleine Artikel für die österreichische Presse umzuarbeiten. Nach ungefähr einem Jahr, im Jahr 1946, zog die Feature Section nach Wien um. Wir arbeiteten nun in einem großen Büro in der Seidengasse, wo auch der *Wiener Kurier* verlegt wurde. Meine Arbeit wurde selbständiger, ich lernte die Grundregeln des Journalismus. An der Demarkationslinie zwischen Wien und Salzburg spritzten uns die Amerikaner DDT in die Nacken, die Russen starrten lange auf unsere Papiere und in unsere Gesichter. Geschichten von Leuten, die sie aus dem Zug holten und die auf Nimmerwiedersehen verschwanden, machten die Runde.

In Wien war ich mit einer Kollegin bei einer Naziwitwe einquartiert. Wir mussten das Bad mit ihr teilen, und sie liebte uns keineswegs. Wir wurden von den Amerikanern verpflegt, Spam und Trockenerbsen dominierten das Menü.

Aber das Leben begann wieder. Alles, alles schien möglich: die verbotenen Bücher zu lesen, im Theater die neuen amerikanischen, französischen und englischen Stücke zu sehen, sich die Fingernägel rot zu lackieren, zu sagen, was man dachte, laut und überall. Ich fing an, kleine Hörspiele für den *Rot-Weiß-Rot*-Sender zu schreiben, und arbeitete in der Redaktion des *Optimisten*, einer guten, aber kurzlebigen literarischen Zeitschrift, wo ich Künstler und Schriftsteller kennenlernte. Hans Weigel, Ilse Aichinger, Ingeborg Bachmann wurden Freunde; Arnold Keyserling führte uns in seinem Studio in die Weisheit des Orients ein, wir fuhren zu den ersten Treffen europäischer Intellektueller, die Otto Molden in Alpbach organisierte. Viktor Frankl, Begründer der Existenzanalyse, ließ mich in seinen Vorlesungen sitzen, in denen er Menschen, die das Kriegserlebnis nicht überwinden konnten, analysierte. Er hatte Auschwitz überlebt, aber seine Familie dort verloren, und betrachtete es als seine Aufgabe, die Überlebenden wieder – ich benutze seine eigenen Worte – dazu zu bringen, „Ja zum Leben zu sagen".

Ich fand eine neue Stellung als österreichische Redakteurin der illustrierten Zeitschrift *Heute*, in München von den Amerikanern herausgegeben. Eine meiner Aufgaben war es, Photographen zum Illustrieren der von mir vorgeschlagenen Reportagen zu finden. Zum ersten Mal studierte ich intensiv Photographien und Bildreportagen, besonders in dem wieder erhältlichen *Life* Magazine, das in seiner Glanzzeit war und die besten Photo-Essays publizierte.

Mein Hauptproblem war, dass die Photos, die mir angeboten wurden, mich nicht inspirierten. Dann kam der Tag, an dem ich Ernst Haas traf, seine Photos sah und begeistert war. Wir fingen an, zusammen zu arbeiten, machten ein paar Stories über Mode und andere mondäne Sujets, die uns nicht am Herzen lagen, von denen wir jedoch fälschlicherweise annahmen, dass sie unseren Redakteuren gefallen würden.

Schließlich entschieden wir uns doch für eine Reportage, die unserer Ansicht nach kaum Gefallen finden würde: Wir verbrachten Tage und Nächte im Ostbahnhof, um die Heimkehr österreichischer Kriegsgefangener aus Russland zu dokumentieren. Jeden Transport erwarteten bange Menschen, Photos vermisster Familienmitglieder in der Hand. Viele, die erwartet wurden, kamen nicht. Die Tragödie des Krieges stand in allen Gesichtern. Wir brachten die Story zu Warren Trabant, dem Chefredakteur von *Heute*, der zu unseren ersten Versuchen nur bemerkt hatte: „This is dreadful. But I think you are talented, just keep going." Dieses Mal war er begeistert, veröffentlichte die Reportage und machte Robert Capa, der 1947 Magnum Photos gegründet hatte, auf uns aufmerksam. Capa kabelte: „Come to Paris." Es war Juli 1949.

Wir packten je einen Koffer und fuhren los, dritter Klasse, ohne zu wissen, dass wir nie wieder auf längere Zeit in Wien leben würden. In meinem Koffer war die alte Contax, die meine Mutter vom Mikroskop abgeschraubt und mir geschenkt hatte. Diese Kamera begleitete mich noch zwei oder drei Jahre lang, ohne je benutzt zu werden.

Ich beschränkte mich weiterhin auf das Beschreiben meiner Beobachtungen, in Tagebüchern, Artikeln und nun bei Magnum mit dem Anfertigen von Bildertexten für die Arbeiten der Mitgliedsphotographen, die aus verschiedenen Teilen der Welt eintrafen.

Oft begleitete ich Ernst Haas und andere Photographen bei Reportagen. Im Büro fing ich eine neue aufregende Arbeit an: die Auswertung der Kontaktseiten jener Photographen, die auf weiten Reisen unterwegs waren und es nicht selbst tun konnten. Kontakte sind die Tagebuchseiten der Photographen, man verfolgt jedes Drücken auf den Auslöser und versucht, den im Augenblick des Photographierens getroffenen Entscheidungen gerecht zu werden, aber auch Schwächeres radikal auszumerzen. Henri Cartier-Bresson war noch im Fernen Osten. Ich war fasziniert von seinen Kontaktseiten, auf denen sich von Bild zu Bild die rigorose Verfolgung eines Ereignisses in klaren geometrischen Kompositionen entfaltete. Ich glaube, ich habe beim Studium der Art, wie er photographierte, selbst photographieren gelernt, ohne je eine Kamera in die Hand genommen zu haben.

1951 heiratete ich einen englischen Journalisten und zog nach London. Ich fühlte mich unsicher; England ist sehr anders als der Kontinent. Es gab unzählige subtile Verhaltensregeln – ich war in einer Shrewsbury-Eaton-Oxford-Gruppe der Gesellschaft gelandet. Es war leicht, sich zu blamieren, und ich zog es oft vor, schweigend dazusitzen und zu beobachten.

Ich hatte plötzlich Zeit und machte alleine endlose Gänge durch London. Zu meinem Erstaunen fing ich an, vieles zu sehen, das meiner Meinung nach photographiert werden sollte. Ich rief mir bekannte Photographen an, aber meine Vorschläge fielen meistens auf taube Ohren, ich bot ja nur Ideen und keine Bezahlung an.

Eines Tages fuhren wir auf kurze Ferien nach Venedig. Als wir ankamen, regnete es. Ich fand das Licht herrlich, die dunklen Silhouetten der durchnässten Passanten wirkten wie choreografiert vor den Marmorwänden. Schließlich hielt ich es nicht mehr aus und rief Robert Capa in Paris an und bat ihn, einen Photographen nach Venedig zu schicken, weil es regnete und man einen wunderbaren Photo-Essay über diese aus dem Wasser geborene Stadt machen könnte. Er antwortete: „Du bist ein Idiot. Wer soll das zahlen, und bis jemand dort hinkommt, hat es wahrscheinlich zu regnen aufgehört. Mach doch endlich mal selbst ein Photo!"

Ich weiß nicht mehr genau, was mich zur Entscheidung trieb. Ich holte die alte Contax aus dem Hotelzimmer, ließ mir in einem Photogeschäft einen Film einlegen, da ich das noch nie getan hatte, hörte aber nicht auf die Ratschläge des Photohändlers, auf Sonnenschein zu warten, denn das war genau das, was ich nicht wollte. Außerdem hatte ich mit Photographen im Regen gearbeitet, und auf der dem Film beigegebenen Gebrauchsanweisung stand: „bei bewölkt 50stel auf 4". Ich fand schnell den Ort, den ich als Beobachtungspunkt für den erhofften Photographen ausgesucht hatte, stellte mich an seiner Stelle hin, wartete, bis sich Menschen, Säulen, Fenster und Tauben in dem Rhythmus befanden, den ich auf einem Photo für gut befunden hätte, und drückte auf den Auslöser. Es war mir sofort klar, dass ich von nun an Photographin sein würde; ich hatte endlich meine Sprache gefunden.

Ich photographierte weiter und war mir freudig bewusst, dass ich nun dem, was ich zu sagen hatte, durch meine Augen Form geben konnte. Ich erinnerte mich an einen Ausspruch Henri Cartier-Bressons: „Ein gutes Photo kommt nur dann zustande, wenn die innere Vision hinter dem geschlossenen Auge sich mit der des offenen Auges hinter dem Sucher im Augenblick des Photographierens deckt."

Ich ging ins Hotel zurück und übte, ohne Photoapparat, mit einem geschlossenen und einem offenen, auf die Straße gerichteten Auge, wann ich auf den Auslöser drücken würde.

Es stellte sich heraus, dass es nicht ganz so einfach war umzusatteln. Wer hätte mir schon ein Photo abgekauft? Alle wussten, dass ich nie photographierte. Also verschwieg ich vorläufig meine Pläne, verkaufte ab und zu einen Artikel, ging viel ins Theater und in die wunderbaren Londoner Museen. Natürlich suchte ich nach jemandem, der mir mehr über Photographieren beibringen konnte. Ich hatte von Simon Guttmann sprechen gehört, er hatte die berühmte deutsche Photoagentur Dephot geleitet und als Erster die Idee des Photo-Essays praktisch angewendet. Unter den Photographen, die

in Deutschland für ihn arbeiteten, war, was ich damals nicht wusste, Robert Capa. Über die Schweiz und Frankreich gelangte Guttmann 1942 oder 1943 nach London, wurde Berater bei *Picture Post*, der besten englischen Illustrierten dieser Zeit, außerdem gründete er seine eigene Photoagentur „Report", für die mehrere Photographen arbeiteten. Einer von ihnen riet mir zu versuchen, dort als Lehrling unterzukommen.

Simon Guttmann galt als barsch und sehr kritisch. Ich ging daher mit Herzklopfen zum ersten Treffen in sein winziges, vollgepfropftes Büro in der Oxford Street. Alles, was ich vorzeigen konnte, waren die Kontaktseiten meiner ersten drei in Venedig aufgenommenen Filme. Er sah sich die Bilder kommentarlos an, dann fragte er, warum und was ich photographieren wollte. Ich murmelte, dass ich Menschen photographieren wollte, in der Vielfalt ihrer Leben. Und dass ich sicher war, dass ich nach dem Leben in Isolation und Krieg in der Photographie meine Sprache gefunden hätte oder wenigstens die beste Art, dem, was ich zu sagen hatte, Ausdruck zu geben. Er sagte: „Sie können bei mir anfangen."

Ich verbrachte ein paar Wochen mit dem Tippen seiner Briefe, an Samstagen beantwortete ich das Telefon und warf Münzen in die Gasheizung, auf der er sein Rasierwasser wärmte, ab und zu kehrte ich auf, mit Sorgfalt die überall aufgetürmten Stapel von Zeitungen umgehend. „Wann bringen Sie mir das Photographieren bei?", wagte ich endlich zu fragen. „Das ist genau das, was ich tue", kam die ungeduldige Antwort. „Lesen Sie mal wirklich, was in meinen Briefen steht. Ich habe Ihnen nur die zu tippen gegeben, die an Photographen oder Redakteure geschrieben sind. Alles, was man über Photographie und Reportage lernen kann, steht drin."

Das stimmte. Außerdem schickte er mich nun oft abends mit meiner Contax in die Straßen Londons. Ich hatte Berichte von Ausstellungseröffnungen und Premierenbesuchern, von Feuern und anderen lokalen Ereignissen zurückzubringen. Eine andere Photographin, die schon länger zu Guttmanns Gruppe gehörte, hatte eine Dunkelkammer, in der ich, von ihm empfohlene Handbücher verwendend, entwickeln und vergrößern lernte. Später verbrachte ich Nächte in Dunkelkammern von Meistertechnikern und beobachtete, wie sie jene Vergrößerungen machten, die für den Photographen ideal sind: sie geben die im Augenblick des Photographierens vorhandene Absicht wieder, indem sie den vom Auge ausgeführten Balanceakt zwischen Licht und Schatten auf dem Papier neu erstehen lassen.

Nach ein paar Monaten erklärte Simon Guttmann, dass ich nun gehen und alleine arbeiten könnte. Er erklärte sich zufrieden mit einer von mir in Paris gemachten Reportage über die Inspektion der Horse Guards durch einen melancholischen Prince of Wales.

Meine neue Leidenschaft half mir, mich aus einer Ehe zu lösen, die von Anfang an nicht besonders geglückt war. Photographieren war mir zu einer Notwendigkeit geworden, und ich wollte es nicht mehr aufgeben. Eine Zeitlang wohnte ich bei Freundinnen in London, erstand eine gebrauchte Leica und begann, unter dem Namen „Egni Tarom" – „Inge Morath" von hinten gelesen – meine Photos an verschiedene Illustrierte zu verkaufen. Eines Tages konnte ich genug Geld zusammenkratzen, um nach Paris zurückzugehen; dort kannte ich billige Hotels, hatte ein paar Freunde, und das Magnum-Büro war in Paris. Ich hatte beschlossen, ein Photo-Essay zu machen, das gut genug war, um damit zu Robert Capa zu gehen und meine Karten auf den Tisch zu legen.

Als Thema wählte ich die „prêtres ouvriers", Arbeiter-priester, die in Paris und anderen Orten Frankreichs hauptsächlich in Fabriken arbeiteten, um wie Missio-nare im eigenen Land ihren Glauben zu verbreiten und den Armen zu helfen. Ich überredete den Redakteur einer katholischen Illustrierten, mir den Auftrag für die Reportage und einen Vorschuss zu geben. Es war ein schwieriges Unternehmen; Erlaubnisse von Ordens-vorstehern mussten eingeholt werden, und die Priester selbst waren erst misstrauisch: Ihre Mission war deli-kat, und obwohl der Kardinal von Paris auf ihrer Seite stand, war der Vatikan dagegen. Wir besprachen, wie wir am besten ihre Arbeit und die Bemühungen ihrer von Simone Weil inspirierten, selbstlosen Helfer zeigen konnten; sie hatten kleine Zentren in armen Vororten gegründet, wo sie Essen verteilten, sich um die Armen kümmerten und sich lediger Mütter annahmen.

Die technischen Bedingungen waren zum Photographie-ren mies, überall war es dunkel: in den Fabriken, in den Zimmern, beim Gang von und zu der Arbeit. Ich lernte, in schlechtem Licht zu arbeiten, es wäre viel zu störend gewesen, Lampen mitzubringen. Nach einer Weile vergaßen sie meine Anwesenheit, was immer das Beste ist. Nach einem hungrigen Monat war ich fertig. Die Illustrierte war zufrieden, und ich ging mit Kopien von Text und Photos zu meinem Rendezvous mit Robert Capa im Magnum-Büro. Er schaute sich alles an, fand den Text gut und fragte endlich: „Wer hat die Photos gemacht? Sie sind gut." – „Ich." – „Du?" -„Ja, ich will Photographin sein."

Capa war der großzügigste aller Photographen. Er über-gab mir von diesem Zeitpunkt an die kleinen Aufträge, die die anderen „Magnum"-Photographen nicht inter-essierten. Der erste war ein *concours des roses* im Parc de Bagatelle. Hundert Dollar Honorar. Ältere Herren in dunklen Anzügen rochen an Rosen, begutachteten Form und Größe und gaben Punkte. Erst stand ich da und wusste nicht recht, wie ich etwas bildlich Aufregendes in einem so unheroischen Thema finden könnte. Aber wenn man beginnt, die Augen aufzumachen, ist alles Leben-dige interessant. Es war ungefähr zu diesem Zeitpunkt, dass Henri Cartier-Bressons Buch *Images à la Sauvette* – auf Englisch *The Decisive Moment* – erschien.

Images à la Sauvette kommt von *se sauver* – sich wie ein illegaler Straßenverkäufer aus dem Blickfeld eines auf-tauchenden „Auge des Gesetzes" zu entfernen, nicht ungleich dem Photographen, der in die Luft schauend und andere Interessen vorgebend davonschlendert und die soeben photographierten Passanten rätseln lässt: „Hat er, oder hat er nicht?".

Henri gab eine wunderbare Imitation dieser Prozedur. Unter den Photographien in diesem Buch war vor allem eine, die mir beibrachte, was es heißt, das Leben zu photographieren und nicht irgendeinem ästhetischen Vorurteil nachzuhängen: Es ist ein Bild von Leuten, die am Ufer der Marne ein Picknick machen. Alle sind dick, die Männer in Hemdsärmeln, die Frauen in Unterröcken. Es hat nicht viel Sinn, Photographien zu beschreiben; ich war tief beeindruckt von der Einfachheit der ange-wendeten Mittel und dem Raffinement des Auges, mit dem Henri dem Genießen eines freien Tages und eines Mahles im Grünen Ausdruck gab. Die anderen Photogra-phen gewöhnten sich allmählich daran, dass ich nun in ihren Reihen arbeitete. Robert Capa schickte mich nach London, eine Reportage über den Film *Moulin Rouge* zu machen, den John Huston in den Shepherd's Bush Stu-dios als Regisseur drehte. Eigentlich hatte Capa selbst diesen Auftrag erhalten. Als er mich an seiner Stelle schickte, sagte er einfach: „you'd better be good".

Ich war noch nie in einem Filmstudio gewesen. Der ein-zige andere anwesende Photograph war Eliot Elisofon; er war hier als Berater für gewisse Farbeffekte, und er war berühmt. Ich versuchte, ihn zu beobachten, aber gerade an diesem Tag saß er hauptsächlich in seinem Sessel. Ein Assistent gab mir ein paar Hinweise: keinen Schatten werfen, nicht auf Kabeln stehen, nicht in die Augenlinie der Schauspieler geraten, nicht zu knipsen, wenn gedreht wird.

John Huston, den meine offensichtliche Ahnungslosig-keit amüsierte, beschloss, hilfreich zu sein, besonders nachdem ich ihm zu seinem großen Vergnügen gestand, dass ich nur eine einzige Rolle Film hatte. Film war damals schwer zu bekommen, und Capa hatte mir gesagt, ich sollte welchen von Elisofon borgen, aber der zeigte sich dazu keineswegs bereit, und dass ich darauf unbedingt was Gutes heimbringen müsste. Er steckte mir drei weitere Rollen Film in die Tasche und winkte mir ab und zu, wenn er fand, dass ich rangehen und photo-graphieren sollte. So ging's gut aus, meine Photos erschienen in verschiedenen Magazinen, ein paar davon auf Doppelseiten.

Ich hatte Glück gehabt, bei dieser Gruppe von Photo-graphen zu landen, die nicht nur durch die Exzellenz ihrer Arbeit, sondern auch durch eine gemeinsame Hoffnung, am Werden einer besseren Welt nach dem Krieg mitzuarbeiten, geprägt war. Robert Capa, der als Photograph für *Life* Magazine durch seine Photos vom Spanischen Bürgerkrieg und der Landung der Alliierten in der Normandie berühmt geworden war, gründete die Photographen-Cooperative 1947 zusammen mit Henri Cartier-Bresson, David Seymour, George Rodger, Bill und Rita Vandivert. Sie nannten sie „Magnum", ein latei-nischer Name, unter dem die aus einem Ungarn, einem Polen, einem Franzosen, einem Engländer und zwei Amerikanern zusammengesetzte Gruppe ihre Ambition ankündigte, der aber außerdem, besonders für Capa, jene große Champagnerflasche symbolisierte, mit der künftige Erfolge zu feiern waren.

Nicht an Gehälter von einer Zeitschrift gebunden, mit einer minimalen Bürostruktur, ließ die Gruppe jeden Photographen seine eigenen Themen finden: Mit dieser Befreiung von der Herrschaft der großen Magazine oder Agenturen hatte Magnum eine neue Art des Reportagemachens erfunden. Wohl die wichtigste Entscheidung Robert Capas war, dass die Negative im Besitz der Photographen und nicht der Illustrierten blieben. Die Harmonie der Intentionen bedeutete keineswegs stilistische Einheit, im Gegenteil: Jeder photographierte, was er wollte, und auf seine Art. Capa traf die großen Entscheidungen. Er liebte einen etwas extravaganten Lebensstil. Wie oft seufzte er bei unserem Anblick: „Wenn ich reich wäre, hielte ich Rennpferde. Ich bin's nicht, drum habe ich Euch."

Er fand Arbeit für uns beim Gin Rummy-Spielen mit Film- oder Zeitungsmogulen in Kitzbühel, Zürs oder Deauville. Er spürte schnell das Potential in Leuten und wusste, sie zu ihrer besten Arbeit anzuspornen. Eine kleine Anekdote illustriert die Atmosphäre dieser Jahre. Henri Cartier-Bresson erzählte sie: „Als ich 1951 von einer dreijährigen Reise in den Fernen Osten zurückkam, erwartete ich, eine beträchtliche Summe auf meinem Konto zu finden, meine Photos von Indien und China waren in der ganzen Welt veröffentlicht worden. Aber Capa sagte: ‚Wir sind fast bankrott. Ich habe inzwischen Dein Geld benützen müssen.' Als ich meine Überraschung ausdrückte, antwortete er, wie immer: ‚Cool it.' Dann schlug er mir zehn verschiedene Ideen für neue Reportagen vor, von denen acht ohne Interesse waren, die neunte gut und die zehnte ausgezeichnet. Also nahm ich meine Kamera wieder in die Hand und ging los."

Robert Capa beschloss, bevor er mich alleine auf große Reportagen schickte, dass ich eine Zeitlang mit Henri Cartier-Bresson zusammenarbeiten sollte, als Researcher, Dolmetscherin, Lehrling. Wir waren hauptsächlich in Europa unterwegs, sprachen selten über Photographie, umso mehr über die Gemälde, die wir uns überall ansahen, über Bücher und über die Surrealisten, deren Denkensart ihn in seiner Jugend stark beeinflusst hatte. Er war sehr an Politik interessiert, und die französische Zeitung Le Monde war obligate tägliche Lektüre.

Ich photographierte meine eigenen Sachen, wenn ich keine Arbeit für ihn zu tun hatte. Damals musste man einen Sucher auf die Kamera stecken, wenn man sich für das eine oder andere Objektiv entscheiden wollte. Henri gab mir einen von Leitz produzierten Sucher namens Vidom, den auch er oft benutzte. Er ging von 35 bis 135 mm. Man konnte, je nach Entfernung des Objekts von der Kamera, die Parallaxe korrigieren. Was Henri an diesem Sucher entzückte, war, dass beim Durchsehen die Sachen auf der umgekehrten Seite erschienen als sie wirklich waren, und dass man außerdem durch eine Drehung alles auf den Kopf gestellt sehen konnte. Nach einigen missglückten Versuchen gewöhnte sich das Auge daran, Szenen auf diese eher abstrakte Weise zu beurteilen: Man lernte die vor sich gehende kontinuierliche Bewegung zu verfolgen, wie sie sich in die vorhandene Geometrie der Szene

einschrieb, und sie im richtigen Moment – oder was man für den richtigen Moment hielt, festzuhalten. Natürlich kann das letzten Endes nur intuitiv sein. „Dein Kompass muss in deinem Auge sein", sagte Henri.

Außerdem lernte ich, wie immer, vom Beobachten. Es war der Photograph, der sich zu bewegen hatte; eine leichte Kniebeuge, eine Neigung des Kopfes ändern die Perspektive, die Treffpunkte von Linien. Langsam wird das alles zur zweiten Natur, und man konzentriert sich auf die Ereignisse.

Ins Büro zurückgekehrt, sahen wir uns gegenseitig unsere Arbeiten an, an Kritik wurde nicht gespart. Es war besonders verpönt, sich über Schwierigkeiten beim Ergattern eines Photos auszulassen, um so etwaige Imperfektionen zu entschuldigen.

Mein erster großer eigener Reportage-Auftrag kam vom Holiday Magazine; ein photographischer Essay über Soho und Mayfair. Ich ging auf eine Zeitlang nach London zurück und fand es aufregend, Eindrücke und Erfahrungen des dort ohne Photoapparat gelebten Lebens nun in Bilder umzuwandeln.

Dann schickte Capa mich nach Spanien. Fast alle Magnum-Photographen arbeiteten an einer neuen, von ihm erfundenen Serie mit dem Titel „Generation Women". „Es ist eine gute Story", sagte er. „Deine Spanierin ist Rechtsanwältin, sie verteidigt arme Frauen in Scheidungsfällen – eine mutige Sache im Franco-Regime. Außerdem ist Spanien das richtige Land für Dich."

Er hatte recht. Spanien wurde zu einem der Länder, in die ich viele Male zurückkehrte, um zu arbeiten. Ich lernte die Sprache schnell und fühlte mich in meinem Element, es war fast wie die Entdeckung einer schon geträumten Erfahrung. Ich hatte die Menschen gern und konnte mit ihnen umgehen. Sie ließen sich photographieren, aber sie wollten auch, dass ich ihnen zuhörte, dass sie mir sagten, was sie wussten, und wir so zusammen ihre Geschichte erzählten. Ohne die Kenntnis der Sprache wäre mir vieles entgangen, und seitdem habe ich immer versucht, die Sprachen der Länder, in denen ich länger arbeiten wollte, zu lernen, inklusive Russisch und Mandarin.

Am 25. Mai 1954 wurde Robert Capa von einer Landmine in Vietnam, wo er den französisch-indochinesischen Konflikt für Life Magazine photographierte, getötet. Es schien unfassbar. Zwei Tage später kam die Nachricht, dass Werner Bischof bei einem Autounfall in den peruanischen Anden tödlich verunglückt war. Robert Capas Bruder Cornell verließ Life Magazine und trat Magnum bei. David Seymour – wir alle nannten ihn Chim – übernahm die Leitung des Büros. Zwei Jahre später wurde Chim beim Photographieren der Suezkrise erschossen. Wir waren entschlossen, in ihrem Sinn weiterzumachen: gute und verantwortliche Arbeit zu liefern, verschiedene Arten zu sehen und zu sein zu tolerieren, Freundschaft zu schätzen und das Leben zu lieben.

Seitdem wurden viele neue Photographen Mitglieder von Magnum. Begabt und eigenwillig schaffen sie weiterhin photographische Essays, die sich gleichwertig neben geschriebener Reportage und dem Fernsehen in dieser sich in ununterbrochenem Fluxus befindlichen Welt mit ihrem omnipräsenten Durst nach Information behaupten.

Für mich hatte die Zeit der großen Reportagen und weiten Reisen begonnen. Ich arbeitete eine Zeitlang im Mittleren Osten, vor allem in Iran, wo 1956 ein paar moderne politische Ideen Fuß zu fassen schienen, zumindest in Teheran. In den Provinzen herrschten die Mullahs. Es war schwierig, dort als Frau zu photographieren. Ich hatte glücklicherweise einen armenischen Chauffeur gefunden, der das Land und die Menschen kannte, vor falschem Benehmen warnte und mir zeigte, den die Kameras verhüllenden Tschador richtig zu drapieren. Ich träumte davon, vom Iran über die Seidenstraße nach China zu gelangen. Diese Idee fiel ins Wasser, und auf das Photographieren in China musste ich noch viele Jahre warten.

Eine Arbeit folgte der anderen – es war wunderbar: Ich folgte den Spuren Spaniens in Mexiko und Südamerika, machte Reportagen über Gold- und Diamantenminen in Südafrika, um nur ein paar zu nennen. Dazwischen machten wir Reportagen über große Spielfilme an Standorten von den argentinischen Anden bis Hollywood. Aus einer Anzahl von Photo-Essays wurden Bücher, eines davon über Flüchtlinge; Yul Brynner und ich photographierten sie für die Vereinten Nationen, von den letzten russischen Lagern in Deutschland bis Gaza.

Ende der fünfziger Jahre setzte ich es mir in den Kopf, die Donau von der Quelle bis zum Delta zu photographieren, um den großen Fluss meiner Heimat besser kennenzulernen. Ich bin jetzt dabei, diese Reise zu wiederholen, und stoße wieder auf Flüchtlinge, die von der Brutalität des Krieges aus der Heimat vertrieben wurden. In der Mitte der fünfziger Jahre gründeten Rosamond und George Bernier in Paris eine neue Kunstzeitschrift namens *L'Œil*. Einer der Redakteure war Robert Delpire, mit dem ich schon ein Buch über die Stierkämpfe in Pamplona gemacht hatte. Er war beim Durchsehen meiner Kontakte auf die Portraits, die ich bei jeder sich bietenden Gelegenheit photographierte, aufmerksam geworden. Da sie ihm gefielen, begann ich eine Serie von Künstlerportraits für *L'Œil* zu photographieren und mit Mary McCarthy an einem Buch über Venedig zu arbeiten.

Meine aus Leicas bestehende Kameraausrüstung wurde um eine großformatige Linhoff für die Reproduktion von Gemälden bereichert.

Ich bereite mich auf eine Portraitaufnahme genauso sorgfältig vor wie auf eine Reise in ein neues Land. Ich lese oder sehe mir die Werke der zu photographierenden Künstler an. Die Vorbereitung ist wichtig, da die Begegnung selbst spontan und kurz ist, ein Gesichtsausdruck ist flüchtig wie ein Schatten. Ich ziehe es bei weitem vor, Menschen an ihrem Arbeits- oder Wohnplatz zu photographieren, in der von ihnen selbst geschaffenen Umgebung. Indem ich sie einlade, sie selbst zu sein, hoffe ich, zum Ausdruck einer inneren Wahrheit zu gelangen. Ich habe eine Zeitlang gebraucht, die Harmonie in schwierigen Gesichtern zu entdecken und ihr mit der Kamera gerecht zu werden.

Eines meiner großen Bedauern aus meiner frühen Arbeitszeit ist, dass ich meine sehr bewunderte Freundin Ingeborg Bachmann nie photographiert habe. Ich hatte Angst, dass ich dem leicht verschwommenen Ausdruck, der ihr Gesicht schön machte, im Photo nicht gerecht würde. Jetzt könnte ich's. Man träumt von versäumten Bildern.

Seit dem Ende der fünfziger Jahre führte meine Arbeit mich oft in die Vereinigten Staaten. Ich wollte schon lange den Karikaturisten Saul Steinberg treffen, dessen Zeichnungen im *New Yorker* mir schon in meiner Wiener Zeit mein Auge für die Vereinigten Staaten geschärft hatten. Er willigte zu einer Portraitsitzung ein und empfing mich in seinem Haus in Manhattan mit einer braunen über seinen Kopf gestülpten Papiertüte, auf die er eine Selbstkarikatur gezeichnet hatte. In der Küche hatte er eine ganze Wand mit anderen Tüten behängt, alle mit Selbstportraits in verschiedenen Stimmungen versehen. Wir begannen ein wunderbares Spiel: Er zeichnete mehr und mehr Portraits von allen möglichen Steinbergiensischen Archetypen auf braune Tüten, ich fand Leute, die drunterpassten, und photographierte sie. Es war interessant zu beobachten, wie schnell sich die Körperstellungen der Modelle dem Gesicht auf der Maske anpassten. Eine Studie in Impersonation: Wie präsentieren wir uns der Welt?

1962 heiratete ich den amerikanischen Dramatiker Arthur Miller. Das Tempo meiner Arbeitsweise wurde dadurch etwas gebremst, aber ich entdeckte schnell, dass der eigene Hinterhof eine Fülle photographischer Entdeckungen bietet. Der Arbeitsrhythmus des Schriftstellers ist anders als der unsere. Er nimmt sich viel Zeit nachzudenken, während er seine Worte formuliert.

Für uns ist Versäumtes unwiderruflich verloren. Aber über die Jahre half mir seine Art, über ein Freignis nachzudenken, zu anderen Sehweisen. Seine Geschichten über die „old timers", unter denen er in seinen ersten Jahren in Connecticut lebte, waren ein Ansporn zur Erforschung meiner neuen Umgebung mit der Kamera. Unser erstes gemeinsames Buch hieß *In the Country* und vereinigte unsere verschiedenen Entdeckungsarten.

In den folgenden dreißig Jahren habe ich, zusammen mit Arthur Miller und alleine, weiter Reisen nach alten Sehnsuchtsländern unternommen, vor allem Russland und China. Durch seine Bemühungen um Schriftsteller in politischen Schwierigkeiten – er war jahrelang der Präsident von PEN International – trafen wir in vielen Ländern Künstler, für deren oft gefährliche Situation ausländische Aufmerksamkeit eine Hilfe war. Natürlich habe ich bei diesen Treffen Portraits gemacht. Beim Spazierengehen in fremden Straßen war es oft auch das Interesse des Schriftstellers für einen Vorgang, das mich zur Entdeckung einer erst nicht offensichtlichen photographischen Lösung brachte.

Manchmal fahre ich immer noch alleine los, Photographieren ist nicht oft mit Komfort verbunden: Aufstehen beim Morgengrauen, Nachtaufnahmen, unbequeme Transportmittel, langes Warten. Aber ich habe gelernt, meine Arbeit mit meinem Leben harmonisch zu verbinden – und so soll es sein. Inzwischen macht unsere Tochter Filme, schreibt ihr eigenes Drehbuch und führt Regie, ihre Generation ist mit dem Film wie mit einer Nabelschnur verbunden. Aber sogar sie, stelle ich befriedigt fest, braucht Standphotos.

In der Photographie selbst gehen gewaltige Veränderungen vor sich, neue Techniken lassen die auf den Rückseiten unserer Photos in den fünfziger Jahren aufgedrückten Stempel: „No cropping, no airbrushing" als eher rührend erscheinen. Digitale Technik kann Photos verändern, ohne Spuren zu hinterlassen, Leute nebeneinanderstellen, die einander nie gesehen haben – aus ist die Zeit, wo man genau wusste, auf welchem Platz im Photo inzwischen in Ungnade gefallene Regierungsmitglieder standen. Da war ein Loch, in einem Fall sogar noch ein Hut, den die Zensur vergessen hatte zu eliminieren. Ich selbst habe Spaß daran, diese neuen Techniken wenigstens zu erlernen, aber sie bleiben Technik für mich, keine Passion. Ich bin immer noch neugierig, ich traue weiter meinen Augen, ich kann es nicht lassen, auf das Leben zu blicken und es zu feiern.

BIOGRAPHIE INGE MORATH

*Photographie ist eine seltsame Sache – trotz der Benut-
zung eines Apparats, also eines technischen Hilfsmittels,
photographieren zwei Photographen, selbst wenn sie
zur gleichen Zeit am selben Ort sind, nie dasselbe.
Die persönliche Sicht ist eigentlich immer von Anfang an
da: Resultat irgendeiner Alchemie von Herkunft, Gefühl,
Tradition und ihrer Ablehnung, Sensibilität und Voyeuris-
mus. Man traut seinem Auge und entblößt seine Seele.
Der Photograph findet unweigerlich die seiner Sicht
angemessene Form.* – Inge Morath

(*Inge Morath. Das Leben als Photographin,* München 1999)

Inge Morath (1923–2002) wurde in Graz geboren. Die
Eltern waren Naturwissenschaftler, ihre Berufstätigkeit
führte sie, als Inge ein kleines Kind war, an unterschied-
liche Labore und Universitäten in Europa. Inge Morath
ging auf französische Schulen, in den 1930er Jahren zog
die Familie nach Darmstadt und dann nach Berlin.

Moraths erste Begegnung mit moderner Malerei war
die von den Nationalsozialisten organisierte Ausstellung *Entartete Kunst* im Jahr 1937, die die öffentliche
Meinung gegen moderne Kunst aufbringen sollte. „Ich
fand einige dieser Gemälde aufregend und verliebte
mich in Franz Marcs *Blaues Pferd*", schrieb Inge Morath
später. „Nur negative Kommentare wurden gebilligt,
und so begann die lange Periode des Schweigens und
Verschweigens."

Nach dem Zweiten Weltkrieg war Morath als Überset-
zerin und Journalistin tätig. 1948 wurde sie von Warren
Trabant für *Heute* engagiert, eine von der US Information
Agency in München herausgegebene Illustrierte. Morath
hatte in Wien Ernst Haas kennengelernt und machte
Trabant auf ihn aufmerksam. Die beiden arbeiteten fort-
an gemeinsam für *Heute*, Morath schrieb Artikel zu den
Bildern von Haas. 1949 wurden Morath und Haas von
Robert Capa eingeladen, für die neu gegründete Agentur
Magnum Photos zu arbeiten. Morath war zunächst als
Redakteurin tätig. Die Arbeit mit den Kontaktbögen des
Gründungsmitglieds Henri Cartier-Bresson faszinierte
sie: „Ich glaube, ich habe beim Studium der Art, wie er
photographierte, selbst photographieren gelernt, ohne
je eine Kamera in die Hand genommen zu haben."

Morath war kurz mit dem britischen Journalisten Lionel
Birch verheiratet und zog 1951 nach London. Im selben
Jahr begann sie auf einer Venedig-Reise zu photo-
graphieren. „Es war mir sofort klar, dass ich von nun an
Photographin sein würde; ich photographierte weiter

und war mir freudig bewusst, dass ich nun dem, was
ich zu sagen hatte, durch meine Augen Form geben
konnte."

Morath ließ sich von Birch scheiden und kehrte
nach Paris zurück, um die Photographie zum Beruf
zu machen.

1955 wurde sie eingeladen, Vollmitglied bei Magnum
Photos zu werden. In den späten 1950er Jahren reiste
sie viel, berichtete aus Europa, dem Nahen Osten, Afri-
ka, den USA und Südamerika für Zeitschriften wie *Holiday*, *Paris Match* und *Vogue*. 1955 veröffentlichte sie,
zusammen mit Robert Delpire, ihr erstes Buch, *Guerre à
la Tristesse* mit Photographien aus Spanien, 1958 folgte
De la Perse à l'Iran mit Photographien aus dem Iran.

Wie viele Magnum-Mitglieder arbeitete Morath als
Still-Photographin an zahlreichen Filmsets. In ihrer
Londoner Zeit hatte sie John Houston kennengelernt
und arbeitete bei mehreren seiner Filme mit. 1960 war
sie am Set von *The Misfits*, einem Blockbuster mit
Marilyn Monroe, Clark Gable und Montgomery Clift,
nach einem Drehbuch von Arthur Miller. Morath lernte
Miller bei den Dreharbeiten von *The Misfits* kennen,
sie heirateten – nach Millers Scheidung von Monroe –
am 17. Februar 1962.

Morath hat bereits in den ersten zehn Jahren ihrer
Tätigkeit als Photographin viel erreicht. Mit Eve Arnold
gehörte sie zu den ersten weiblichen Mitgliedern von
Magnum Photos, einer bis heute von Männern dominierten Organisation. In der Presse wurde viel über das
spielerisch-surrealistische Element geschrieben, das
Moraths Werk aus dieser Zeit charakterisiert. Es war
durch einen fundamentalen Humanismus motiviert und
von der Erfahrung des Krieges und dessen anhaltendem
Schatten über Nachkriegseuropa geprägt. Diese Motivation wächst im reifen Werk zu einem Motiv heran,
wenn Morath die Widerstandskraft des menschlichen
Geistes in extremen Zwangslagen dokumentiert, aber
auch seine Manifestationen in Ekstase und Freude.

Ingeborg Morath Miller starb 2002, mit 78 Jahren, an
Krebs. Zu Ehren ihrer Kollegin gründeten die Mitglieder von Magnum Photo noch im selben Jahr den Inge
Morath Award, er wird von der Inge Morath Foundation
in Kooperation mit der Magnum Foundation, New York,
verwaltet. Das Inge Morath-Archiv wurde im Jahr 2014
von der Beinecke Library at Yale University erworben
und ist für Forschungszwecke zugänglich.

110 FRANKREICH. Paris. Ingrid Bergman und Anthony Perkins am Set von *Goodbye Again*, 1960.

111 FRANKREICH. Paris. Françoise Sagan mit Ingrid Bergman und Yves Montand, 1960.

112 FRANKREICH. Paris. Regisseur Anatole Litvak, Anthony Perkins, Ingrid Bergman und Yves Montand am Set von *Goodbye Again*, 1960.

113 FRANKREICH. Paris. Ingrid Bergman am Set von *Goodbye Again*, 1960.

114 USA. New York, NY. John Malkovich, Kate Reid, Dustin Hoffman und Steven Lang in der Broadway-Produktion von Arthur Millers *Death of a Salesman*, 1984.

115 USA. New York, NY. Dustin Hoffman und Regisseur Volker Schlöndorff bei den Dreharbeiten zu *Death of a Salesman*. 1985.

116 ENGLAND. José Ferrer als Toulouse Lautrec mit Regisseur John Huston am Set von *Moulin Rouge*, 1953.

117 ENGLAND. Zsa Zsa Gabor bei den Dreharbeiten zu *Moulin Rouge*, 1953.

118-120 SPANIEN. Madrid. Gina Lollobrigida am Set von *Solomon and Sheba*, Regie King Vidor, 1958.

121 ARGENTINIEN. Salta. Christine Kaufmann bei den Dreharbeiten von *Taras Bulba*, Regie J. Lee Thompson, 1961.

122–123 ARGENTINIEN. Salta. Christine Kaufmann, 1961.

124 ARGENTINIEN. Salta. Yul Brynner und Christine Kaufmann in der Maske, am Set von *Taras Bulba*, 1961.

125–126 ARGENTINIEN. Salta. Yul Brynner am Set von *Taras Bulba*, 1961.

127 ARGENTINIEN. Salta. Inge Morath am Set von *Taras Bulba*. Photograph unbekannt, 1961.

128 ARGENTINIEN. Salta. Tony Curtis am Set von *Taras Bulba*, 1961.

129 USA. Reno, NV. Drehbuchautor Arthur Miller und Regisseur John Huston bei den Dreharbeiten zu *The Misfits*, 1960.

130 USA. Reno, NV. Clark Gable bei den Dreharbeiten zu *The Misfits*, 1960.

131 USA. Reno, NV. Marilyn Monroe und Eli Wallach proben eine Szene für *The Misfits*, 1960.

132 USA. Reno, NV. Clark Gable und Marilyn Monroe am Set von *The Misfits*, 1960.

133 USA. Reno, NV. John Huston, Marilyn Monroe und Arthur Miller am Set von *The Misfits*, 1960.

134–139 USA. Reno, NV. Marilyn Monroe und Eli Wallach proben eine Tanzszene für *The Misfits*, 1960.

140 USA. Reno, NV. Clark Gable bei den Dreharbeiten zu *The Misfits*, 1960.

141 USA. Reno, NV. Marylin Monroe und Arthur Miller bei den Dreharbeiten zu *The Misfits*, 1960.

142 USA. Reno, NV. Marilyn Monroe nach einem Drehtag für *The Misfits*, 1960.

143–144 USA. Reno, NV. Marilyn Monroe am Set von *The Misfits*, 1960.

145-148 USA. Reno, NV, 1960.

FRANKREICH, SPANIEN, RUSSLAND, IRAN, CHINA

149 FRANKREICH. Paris. Place de Furstemberg, 1958.

150 FRANKREICH. Paris. Vor der Auktion bei Drouot, 1954.

151 FRANKREICH. Enghien-les-Bains, 1954.

152 FRANKREICH. Paris, 1953.

153 FRANKREICH. Paris. Rue Saint Paul, 1955.

154 FRANKREICH. Paris, 1958.

155 FRANKREICH. Paris, 1955.

156–157 FRANKREICH. Paris, 1956.

158 FRANKREICH. Paris, 1958.

159 SPANIEN. Madrid. Mercedes Fórmica, Anwältin und Schriftstellerin. 1955.

160 SPANIEN. Madrid. Calle Mayor, Sonntagnachmittag, 1992.

161–163 SPANIEN. Pamplona. Fiesta da San Fermin, 1954.

164 SPANIEN. Pamplona. 1954.

165 SPANIEN. Toledo. Straße hinter der Kathedrale, 1961.

166 SPANIEN. Pamplona. Während der Fiesta da San Fermin stehen Kran-kenhausbetten für Verletzte bereit, 1954.

167 SPANIEN. La Alberca. Später Samstagnachmittag auf dem Dorfplatz, 1955.

168 SPANIEN. Cordoba. Café in einem Dorf, 1962.

169–173 SPANIEN. Pamplona. Fiesta da San Fermin. 1954.

174 SPANIEN. Pamplona. Pferdemarkt, 1954.

175 SPANIEN. Almonte. Andalusien. Romeria del Rocio. Siesta des Ochsentreibers, 1955.

176 SPANIEN. Pamplona. 1954.

177–178 SPANIEN. Pamplona. Fiesta da San Fermin. Zuschauer der Corrida, 1954.

179 SPANIEN. Pamplona. Fiesta da San Fermin. Amateure dürfen in die Arena, 1954.

180 SPANIEN. Madrid. Einzug der Picadores zu Beginn der Corrida. Plaza de Toros während der Feria de San Isidro, 1955.

181 SPANIEN. Pamplona. Luis Miguel Dominguin, 1957.

182 SPANIEN. Pamplona. Fiesta da San Fermin. Der Torero César Girón, 1954.

183 UdSSR. Leningrad. Der Schriftsteller Joseph Brodsky auf dem Dach der Peter- und-Paul-Festung, ehemals ein zaristisches Gefängnis, 1967.

184 UdSSR. Moskau. Roter Platz. Menschenschlange vor dem Eingang ins Lenin-Mausoleum. 1965.

185 UdSSR. Kloster Sagorsk. Sonntagsmesse, 1988.

186 UdSSR. Pereslawl-Salessky. Verlassenes Kloster, 1967.

187 UdSSR. Leningrad. Torweg und Hof, wie Dostojewski ihn auf dem Weg von Raskolnikows Kammer zur Wohnung der Pfandleiherin in *Schuld und Sühne* beschreibt, 1967.

188 UdSSR. Moskau. Ein kleines Mädchen wartet auf die Gäste der Eltern. 1989.

189 UdSSR. Die Bahn Lomonosov – Leningrad. Ein Ehepaar fährt mit Taschen voller Lebensmittel von der Datscha nach Hause, 1989.

190 UdSSR. Leningrad. Blick aus dem Winter-Palast, 1965.

191 UdSSR. Moskau. Die Primaballerina Maia Plissezkaja im Bolshoi Theater, 1967.

192 IRAN. Qum. Inge Morath. Photograph unbekannt, 1956.

193 IRAN. Persepolis. Säulen der Apadana, 1956.

194 IRAN. Isfahan. Maidan-i-Shah, Hauptplatz von Isfahan, 1956.

195–196 IRAN. Yazd. 1956.

197 IRAN. Forschungslabor in der Raffinerie von Abadan, 1956.

198 IRAN. Abadan. Britische und iranische Techniker während der Nachtschicht im Kontrollraum des Catalytic Cracker, 1956.

199 IRAN. Industriegelände am Stadt-rand von Teheran. In der Ferne das schneebedeckte Elburs-Gebirge, 1956.

200 CHINA. Beijing. Darstellerin in Arthur Millers Drama *Death of a Salesman* am Volkskunsttheater Beijing, 1983.

201 CHINA. Beijing. Probe der Kampf-szene in *Death of a Salesman*, Volkskunsttheater, 1983.

202 CHINA. Beijing. *Death of a Salesman* am Volkskunsttheater, 1983.

203 CHINA. Beijing. Arthur Miller, Ying Ruocheng und weitere Darsteller der *Death of a Salesman*-Produktion am Volkskunsttheater, 1983.

204 CHINA. Beijing. Autor Arthur Miller beim Besuch des Capitol Theater. Rechts von Miller Chinas bekanntes-ter Theaterautor Cao Yu, 1978.

205 CHINA. Beijing. *Death of a Salesman* am Volkskunsttheater. Arthur Miller und Ying Ruocheng, 1983.

206 CHINA. Beijing. *Death of a Salesman* am Volkskunsttheater. Arthur Miller, 1983.

207 CHINA. Beijing. *Death of a Salesman* am Volkskunsttheater. Links Ying Ruocheng, 1983.

208 CHINA. Beijing. *Death of a Salesman* am Volkskunsttheater. Arthur Miller (Mitte), Ying Ruocheng (vorne rechts), 1983.

209 CHINA. Soldaten an einer Maitreya-Skulptur aus der Yuan-Dynastie. Westsee bei Hangzhou, 1978.

210 CHINA. Hangzhou. Arthur Miller mit seinem Dolmetscher Su Guang, 1978.

211 CHINA. Beijing. Morgen auf der Chang'an Avenue, 1978.

212 CHINA. Guilin. 1978.

IMPRINT / IMPRESSUM

This catalog is published in conjunction with the exhibition /
Diese Publikation erscheint anlässlich der Ausstellung

INGE MORATH. HOMMAGE
Kunstfoyer der Versicherungskammer Kulturstiftung, München
21. Dezember 2022 bis 1. Mai 2023

This catalog and exhibition were made possible due to
collaboration with Inge Morath Estate, its representative
Sana Manzoor as well as Anna-Patricia Kahn.

EDITORS / HERAUSGEBER
Isabel Siben
Anna-Patricia Kahn

AUTHORS / AUTOREN
Inge Morath
Rebecca Miller

COPYEDITING / LEKTORAT
Marion Kagerer

TRANSLATIONS / ÜBERSETZUNGEN
Marion Kagerer

GRAPHIC DESIGN AND TYPESETTING /
GRAFISCHE GESTALTUNG UND SATZ
Valerie Kiock graphic design

PAPER / PAPIER
150 gsm Condat Perigord matt

PRINTING / DRUCK
Longo, Bozen

Published by / Erschienen im
Schirmer/Mosel Verlag

ISBN 978-3-8296-0972-2

A Schirmer/Mosel Production
www.schirmer-mosel.com